PROBABLE CAUSE
RE-THINKING
THE JFK PLOT
Revised Edition 2020

Robin Haines

GoToPublish LLC
1-888-337-1724
www.gotopublish.com
info@gotopublish.com

CONTENTS

PREFACE

Was the JFK assassination the result of a random crime or a politically motivated conspiracy?

Perhaps it was a legitimate covert intelligence operation of the US government. Could it be that JFK wasn't murdered and his death was staged to appear to be a homicide?

The author outlines a moral motive for the assassination and an explanation in the way the assassination was staged. The focus of this alternative theory revolves primarily around three men, whom she claims are the most important figures involved in planning and executing the death of JFK. There apparently were many other people linked to this, but she discusses these three people—the main man who ran the operation and the other two who basically planned it. Before their deaths, they both confessed to their involvement and that they planned the assassination. At the time when this theory was first written during the early 1980s, most of these people were still living; however, by now they are deceased.

The author claims the president voluntarily cooperated with his senior intelligence officers in a massive deception, which was carried out as a means of civil defense.

The possibility does exist that JFK had to die in order to save America. The *Deception in Dallas* may have been the only alternative to nuclear war.

In this book, the author challenges both the Warren Commission findings as well as some ideas which have been presented by the criminal conspiracy theorists.

CHAPTER ONE
Why They Thought the JFK Assassination Was Necessary

This book is intended to send a powerful message to the American people, providing an alternative theory about the assassination of President John F. Kennedy.

On November 29, 1963, just one week after the assassination of President John F. Kennedy, President Lyndon Johnson appointed a seven-member panel called the Warren Commission to investigate the Kennedy assassination. It was headed by Chief Justice of the Supreme Court Earl Warren. In September of 1964, this panel released its findings.

They concluded that Lee Harvey Oswald acted alone. They claimed he fired three shots from a sixth-floor window of a book depository (source: Wikipedia, public domain).

In 1991, Oliver Stone's film, *JFK: The Story That Won't Go Away*, lead to an act of Congress, which was passed in 1992, called the President John F. Kennedy Records Collection Act. By now, it has resulted in the declassification of many of the files and documents of this era.

As of this writing, the controversy still lies between the Warren Report and the various conspiracy theories. Books have been written defending the Warren Report such as *Reclaiming History* by Vincent Bugliosi and *Case Closed* by Gerald Posner. While there are numerous conspiracy theories, the most commonly believed are those presented in the Oliver Stone movie and the book *Blood, Money, & Power* by Barr McClellan.

President Clinton appointed a five-member panel called the Federal Assassinations Records Review Board to study these files and documents. In 1998, the member of this panel stated that they couldn't find any evidence to indicate a conspiracy had taken place.

Most people are still unconvinced. They believe our government is still being dishonest with them about the circumstances that surround this president's death.

The majority of the American people believe that there was a politically motivated criminal conspiracy within the United States government to murder JFK in Dallas. Only a small minority believe the Warren Commission Report.

It can be very frightening to an average person to have something like this happen and have so much information withheld from them by their government.

It can be even more disturbing to have other evidence surface at a later time, with the more recently disclosed evidence being deliberately slanted, distorted, and misrepresented in such a manner as to give the impression that this was done with corrupt and malicious intent.

There is an overwhelming amount of evidence which has been brought forth over the decades, making intelligence involvement in this matter apparent to the average person. On the other hand, it is my position that the criminal conspiracy theorists have been distorting, misconstruing, misrepresenting, and politicizing this information pertaining to these tragic events. Without a doubt, this assassination was the main event of a series of events which were orchestrated and manipulated from within the US government.

I want to prove that the Kennedy assassination was not the result of a criminal conspiracy by the result of a massive intelligence deception that was staged from within the United States government. It is the first time in modern history that a political assassination has ever been successfully carried out as an act of civil defense. I have evidence that can prove beyond a shadow of a doubt that the whole government is behind this and that it was done for a good reason.

The purpose of writing this book is to convince people that this assassination was a responsible action based on sound judgment. Just because evidence has surfaced making intelligence involvement apparent to the average person does not mean their intentions were criminal. There were some serious problems with this president's behavior and conduct, which would have given these intelligence officers of the era what they considered to be a just provocation for an action of this nature.

They have been calling this a conspiracy. I find that word inappropriate, since a conspiracy is a plot consisting of more than one person to do something evil, treacherous, or sinister. Believe it or not, that is not what we are dealing with here.

Political assassination is, for the most part, a terrible thing. It is usually carried out with corrupt and malicious intent. It is certainly not something people should resort to as a means of solving problems.

However, there are circumstances, which may arise, where it can be an effective means of civil defense. This is the only instance in which would ever justify an assassination when it is the only alternative to war. Even then, it should be used as a last resort.

Dan Rather was the first to link E. Howard Hunt with the assassination of the CBS Radio Broadcast called *Thinking the Unthinkable*. This was in 1973.

There was enough evidence, as of 1979, to prove that E. Howard Hunt and David Atlee Phillips planned the staging of the Kennedy assassination. There were others like James Jesus Angleton, Cord Meyer, David Morales, William Harvey, Frank Sturgis, etc.

However, I do not want to get into too much depth or detail. My objective is to keep this short and simple. I will not get into all the people who have been linked to the JFK assassination one way or another because I do not want this book to be too long.

As the conspiracy theorists have claimed, there was enough evidence to arrest these people by the late 1970s. My book will explain why that action was never taken.

However, as I said earlier, it is not really a crime under the circumstances for which they should be arrested, indicted, or prosecuted. I'm certain by now that Richard Helms is going to be the main man behind this. I'm sure he was the man who led the others and was running the show at the top. Many people believe that Lyndon Johnson was the man who was behind it. Others see the director of the FBI J. Edgar Hoover as being the man who was behind it. I am aware of the evidence indicating that Johnson and Hoover were definitely involved, and I do believe the evidence linking them to this assassination is credible. However, based on my research, I am convinced that Richard Helms is going to be the man whom this idea originated.

Helms is the only man, who would have been in a high enough position within the government at the time, who would have been capable of this. He's the only one who had the background in espionage to know how to stage a deception like this; he wouldn't have had any religious or moral convictions that would have prevented him from doing this. He also had direct, personal access to the president and was in a position where he had complete control over which information reached the Warren Commission. He is also the only man whose name is on the cover of some of the files. He was the director of plans (which is the director of operations today).

The person who holds this position has the responsibility of explaining a proposed operation to the president.

He has to convince the president that an operation is necessary and justified and get the president's written approval of the plan. This is usually a routine part of the DO's job more so than it is. The DCI's Richard Helms held that position at the time. I believe that either of them can get one.

However, I want to prove that our government did this to protect us and not to terrorize us. This was an intelligence deception designed to look like a politically motivated assassination, but the motives behind it are above and beyond politics.

They just wanted it to appear as though the nations most admired and respected president was gunned down in cold blood by a crazed assassin for no apparent reason other than his own personal unhappiness and psychological problems. They wanted people to believe who were living in the country at the time that Kennedy had been the victim of a crime! His death was brilliantly staged to appear to be a homicide, but it was really a deception and a diversion, which was used to achieve an objective pertaining to our civil defense.

This is not the same thing as a conspiracy to murder him.

Eventually, the cause of this president's death will be changed. It will be looked upon as an act of clandestine espionage to prevent a major war from breaking out between nations. It might be considered an unconventional alternative to war or an act of civil defense to protect the civilian populations from catastrophic consequences. Today they would call this a massive black operation or a major national security event.

This was not done without the president's knowledge and consent, and the vice president had also been informed about it so that he would be prepared to assume the presidency afterward. The Johnson Tapes, which were declassified in the mid-1990s, revealed evidenced of Lyndon Johnson's knowledge of the reason for this assassination. He called Rose Kennedy on the phone on November 22, 1963 to express his condolence. His opening words were "You know, Rose, we're lucky!" Then he stuttered and choked, as if trying to swallow his words, and then he said, "We were lucky to have had your son as long as we did!"

There has been much evidence, which has been exposed in more recent years, which overwhelmingly indicates that Vice President Johnson played a role in planning and running this operation. This does not mean that he was the man behind it.

The United States has enjoyed more domestic national security than any other country on the face of the earth. The twentieth century has been the most violent the world has ever seen. Perhaps as many as 200,000 million people have lost their lives, just during this century due to wars, famines, and other tragedies, caused by corrupt governments and mental illnesses in high places.

Our troops have been sent abroad to engage in foreign conflicts, but America has always remained safe from the ravages of war, which have devastated other nations.

During the forty years when we had an arms race with the Soviet Union, the missiles never launched.

The only reason why the birds never flew is because our intelligence officers did this.

They had to take the life of one man, which ended up costing a few lives, to save the lives of millions of innocent people who surely would have perished.

This is the first time a United States president had to leave office in a box to preserve world peace and to maintain the safety and security of the United States. But believe me, this was the reason our government did this, not for any of the ruthless, corrupt, malicious reasons, which were given in the conspiracy books and in the Oliver Stone movie *JFK*!

I am sure that there were intelligence reports that were put on the desks of these senior executives at the CIA. From what I know about how these federal agencies operate, I am pretty sure that what was in these reports is what is going to be behind the JFK assassination. It was nothing personal or political.

JFK has what psychoanalysts today call dissocial criminal reactive disorder. At least, this is the technical term for what commonly call the *Godfather II* syndrome of the second-generation Mafia mentality. It is a psychopathic personality disorder, which is caused by growing up in a family that is either involved with organized crime or of some other form of criminal activity. It produces an individual who will have a completely split personality, depending on who they are with, especially when it comes to their character. In other words, it is a character disorder. Today, psychiatrists and psychologists may call this an antisocial reactive disorder or an antisocial criminal reactive disorder.

For more information on that subject, please look up dissocial criminal reactive disorder, psychopathic personality, abnormal personality development, abnormal psychology, social psychology, criminal psychology, compulsive sexual behavior, or sexual addition caused by psychopathic personality.

This is what caused the "dark side of Camelot" controversy. The condition is caused environmentally, and it is also an environmental factor which triggers it off, causing the individual to be like a chameleon. They will be a different person at different times, like Dr. Jekyll and Mr. Hyde.

Joseph Kennedy allegedly made his millions in the Irish Syndicate during prohibition. These years were the most formative and most impressionable years of the young Kennedy boy's lives. I believe that what they might have seen going on in their own home during these early childhood years gave them a distorted perception of morality. They saw their father living in two worlds, two different societies, which gave them the idea that society is split in two: criminal society and polite, civilized, legitimate society.

Therefore, they learned to behave differently, depending on whether they were in the company of respectable people who were legitimate or if they were in the company of criminals, whores, and molls, who were of the underworld. I believe this psychopathic personality disorder is the underlying cause for Kennedy's sexual addiction and his notorious womanizing. Psychopaths have problems achieving and experiencing human warmth and closeness in relationships. I can only conclude that this hunger for intimacy is what caused his insatiable need for sex. This condition made him an extremely dangerous man in the position he had obtained in our government.

Although he has been educated at Harvard and had written Pulitzer Prize–winning books, he was not able to reason morally and make morally responsible decisions that a president has to make in the White House. His domestic policies and programs were extremely benevolent for the American people. However, his foreign policy decisions were all acts of war and serious violations of international law.

There are some things that will just provoke a verbal condemnation for other governments. There are other things that will cause sanctions or perhaps an economic embargo to be placed on a country by other countries, then there are some violations of international law which are justifications for war to be declared on a country by another country or other countries.

When you study Kennedy's approach to foreign affairs, you will find that everything he did were acts of war against sovereign nations, which were significant enough to provoke war to be declared on the United States. It is just that what the Soviets did not know at the time could not bother them. This information did not become known until the middle of the 1970s.

The president was also taking many small personal vacations from the White House. Very often, his wife did not know where he was, and neither did the White House staff. We all know by now what he was doing when he went away. Since he certainly was not going away on official business, he would not sign a temporary transfer of power over to the vice president. Therefore, if a national crisis had arisen while he was away, the vice president would not have been able to act on his behalf.

Therefore, we were completely without a president at times during the most dangerous period in history.

The policies and tactics of the Kennedy administration were inviting the Soviets to a nuking party on American soil. Then, he was leaving his post and traveling around the country to see his girlfriends. If the Russians had attacked us, they would have been annihilating our cities and killing millions of our people. Yet we would not have been able to launch one single missile in our own defense. Eventually, NATO would have come in, but millions of innocent people would have perished.

Most people living today do not seem to be aware of the fact that nuclear war was actually declared on the United States by the Soviet Union on October 27,1962. The order to fire nuclear weapons was given to the captain of a Soviet submarine. His name was Vasili Arkhipov. An American Air Force pilot named Rudolph Anderson was also on a mission where he was ordered to fire WMDs during the Cuban Missile Crisis. This information was declassified in 2015. I did not use it in the earlier additions of this book. The American people were told that Rudolf Anderson's plane was armed only with a camera and that he was on a surveillance mission over Cuba. Evidence was declassified in 2015, indicating this pilot had been ordered to deliver a payload of nuclear-tipped air-to-surface missiles into the missile sites in Cuba. His plane was shot down by the Soviets before he could carry out his mission. If you search the internet today, you will only find articles saying that his plane was unarmed. However, I read something about documents having been declassified, saying that his plane was armed with nuke-tipped ASMs and that is why his plane was shot down. Sometimes information might be declassified and then reclassified. I think this is what happened. The Anderson incident occurred on October 27, 1962. He was the only casualty of the Cuban Missile Crisis.

There is only person one in the United States government who can order or authorize the use of nuclear weapons, and that person is the president of the United States.

On the Soviet side, Captain Arkhipov defied the orders of his commanding officer and refused to fire when he was ordered to. If he had obeyed, it probably would have been the end of the world. These senior intelligence officers had to assume that the next time that order was given, they would go through with it.

Kennedy also suffered from Addison's disease. Apparently, his adrenal glands were burned out. This caused him to suffer severe pain in his lower back. He had become addicted to painkillers. He was reported to have used cocaine and smoked marijuana. There is evidence that he was not only swallowing painkiller pills, but he was also being injected with large doses of painkillers by Dr. Maxwell Jacobson, also known as Dr. Feel Good.

He was being injected with amphetamines and methamphetamines, which are hallucinogenic. There are also reports of him having been given shots of steroids, which also affect mental and emotional health. There was also a drug he was being given to sleep called Nembutal. It is believed that his drug also causes lingering side effects.

Much has been documented about JFK having tripped on LSD with his mistress Mary Meyer. She was the ex-wife of the senior intelligence officer Cord Meyer. Apparently, she was able to obtain the acid from Dr. Timothy Leary. He had been working for the CIA on the MKUltra mind control program. Reportedly, she had been able to make this connection through her ex-husband.

In addition to the psychopathic criminal reactive disorder, the use of these drugs would have further impaired his judgment. This was also causing him to have other psychological problems in addition to the ones he already had.

The man was mentally as well as physically ill to the point where he was unable to function. He could not execute the responsibilities of the office in a morally responsible manner. He was a clear and present danger, which is a direct and immediate threat to the safety and security of the United States.

It could have been perceived that not one man, woman, or child living on the face of the earth was safe as long as that man was in that office. The situation was a nuclear Pearl Harbor, just waiting to happen, asking to happen, begging to happen.

What Kennedy was doing that was so bad they might have felt they had to kill him was that he was putting contracts out on leaders of foreign governments. He had ordered governments illegally overthrown by force and committed our troops to an illegal war we could not possibly win. If the Soviets had even found out through their intelligence that attempts were being made on the life of Fidel Castro, the birds would have flown and everyone would have been toast!

I strongly disagree with the motive that was given for this in the Oliver Stone movie *JFK* that people in our government had Kennedy killed so they could prolong and escalate the Vietnam War. The United States government would not execute its own head of state to prolong a war.

The people who support the idea that Kennedy was killed because he changed his position on Vietnam are being irrational. I do feel compelled to challenge this theory.

For one thing, the law would not have allowed JFK to bring the troops home with an executive order. The president can commit troops to a foreign conflict with an executive order, but he wouldn't be able to end the military operation just by signing another executive order.

He would have had to propose a bill and go through Congress. However, he wouldn't have been very likely to succeed. If he had lived long enough, the law would have allowed him to try. However, Congress would have voted it down.

I believe on October 2 of 1963, JFK signed a document asking for a thousand troops to be removed from Vietnam and a complete pullout by 1965. This is what the conspiracy theorists are going with as the reason for his assassination.

However, our governments policy at the time was that we had to prove that we would not back down on our commitments to foreign governments—no matter how small the country, no matter how far away. If this plan had been implemented, it would have shown the world that we were backing away from our commitment to Vietnam.

This was a commitment on behalf of the United States government. It's not something the president can revoke by himself. For this reason, Congress would not have supported this. If he did, he would have done it illegally.

In the early 1960s, the Vietnam War was very popular, and the support for this war was very strong in Congress and generally among the American people. It did not become an unpopular war until the later sixties. Even then, the support was still too strong in Congress for withdrawal to be an option.

The other reason this document indicating JFK's intent to end the Vietnam war was signed on October 2 of 1963. The evidence which has been brought forth by the conspiracy theorists indicates that his assassination was being planned long before that. An operation of this scope and magnitude was not brought about in a short fifty-eight days.

So, the criminal conspiracy theorists' idea that JFK was assassinated because he flip-flopped on Vietnam does not work. I am sure that toward the end of his life, JFK had a lot of very deep and serious regrets. He certainly did see where committing troops to Vietnam had been a mistake. He did want to bring them home. This I am not disputing. However, a competent president would have known better than to have committed troops to the Vietnam conflict in the first place.

However, the United Government would go to this length to prevent a war, especially if it was going to be major war and a nuclear war, which probably would have been the end of the world.

CHAPTER TWO

How They Might Have Done It, Basically

My theory shows how this operation was staged in order to make it look like one man was acting alone. I see Oswald as one of the assassins but not the only assassin at Dealey Plaza. At first, I believed Oswald was to be the only assassin. After a few years I was convinced that other shots were fired. I was only seven years old when JFK was elected president. I was ten when he was assassinated and eleven when the Warren Report came out. I did believe the story that was told in the Warren Report. I was only a child. I remembered hearing the adults talking about it. The story which was told in the Warren Report is what seemed like had happened. At the time, I could not think of a reason that our own government would do something like this to our own president. Just before the Watergate scandal in the late 1969 and very early 1970s, I was convinced that other gunmen were present. I thought there were only two other gunmen. I believed that one of the other gunmen caused the throat wound in JFK and that the other caused the multiple bullet fragments in Gov. John

Connolly's wrist. I still saw Oswald as the assassin who killed JFK with the third shot fired from his old WWI-era bolt action gun. I was under the impression that the people who were involved with the Guy Banister Detective Agency in New Orleans were behind it and that it didn't go any further than them. This is what I believed just before the Watergate scandal.

An early theory of mine was that the knoll shots were a mistake. At first, I did suspect that the grassy knoll assassins decided to fire on the car at the last minute when they weren't supposed to. I did not think the knoll shots were a part of the plan. However, I quickly tossed this idea aside.

In the fall of 2009, I began an email correspondence with Professor Jim Fetzer. He is now retired from University of Minnesota. He writes articles for the Veterans Today website. He has written many books on the subject of the JFK plot.

We found that we agree about many things. However, he still stands firmly behind the idea that Oswald was framed. Some conspiracy theorists believe that Oswald never left the lunchroom. Professor Fetzer believes Oswald was standing in the front doorway of the book depository. His position is that a photograph was altered by superimposing Bill Lovelady's head onto Oswald's body. The photography expert and analyst Robert Groden and Robert D. Morningstar are also strongly convinced that Oswald is the doorway man in the Altgens photograph.

Jim Fetzer also strongly disagrees with me about the president having been involved with his own assassination. He believes documents were signed by other people in other positions but that the president did not sign an executive order or authorization for this. When I published my book with Author House in 2007, the people in the JFK Assassination Community really tore my book up and mocked it because I said that JFK had signed executive orders, along with documents which were signed by other high-level government officials. I did have some mistakes in this version of my book which I have since corrected.

However, I noticed the main problem they had with my book is that I said that there is evidence that the president himself was involved and must have signed some documents which completed a cover. I believe that this is the reason why these people were able to operate above the law and not be prosecuted.

If you were one of these people, you would want to make sure that you would die as a very old man in a warm bed. You would make sure that no matter how much evidence conspiracy theorists and independent researchers found of your involvement, no action would be taken against you through the legal system.

I do not believe this case was just built around Oswald, who was just an innocent patsy whom they framed while other people did all the killing. I don't think Oswald was in the lunchroom and that men walked into the building, went up on the roof, and shot the president without being seen by anyone. It would have been very difficult and extremely risky for anyone to manufacture and then plant the evidence found at the sniper's nest without being seen.

There were too many people who saw a man in the sixth-floor window with a rifle who fit Oswald's description. Robert McNeill was standing with Sergeant Harkness while four witnesses were describing the man they saw in the window with the gun. The three shots which were fired from the sixth-floor window known as the sniper's lair were recorded on a Dictaphone tape in in the Dallas police station.

If the government had framed Oswald with false evidence, there would have been one shot from one gun. It would have been fired from one location. The CIA would have had one of their snipers steal Oswald's gun from the Paine garage. He would have taken it to the sixth floor of that book depository and fired one shot. Then the party would have been over for JFK, with just one single shot. No one would have seen this person enter the building and no one would have seen him leave.

I believe that the more evidence the conspiracy theorists and independent investigators found of other shots and other gunmen indicates that they did use Oswald as one of the shooters. This is why they needed the other gunmen there in order to make sure this very sick president with the split personality disorder was dead.

Then, they went to work altering and tampering with the evidence to try to cover up for the other shots. However, it would take years and years for the presence of other gunmen to be discovered.

However, if Oswald had not been in the window at the time of the assassination firing on the motorcade, there are a lot of places he could have turned up. I can think of about a hundred things that could have happened. If any one of them did, the whole cover on this operation would have been blown that day.

(Photograph courtesy of Saint John Hunt. It is also public domain.)

All five of E. Howard Hunt's children swear Hunt is in this picture as one of the three tramps. The dark-haired woman in the background holding her hand over her mouth they identify as their late mother Dorothy. This picture was taken when the three tramps were released from custody. A man by the name of Chauncy Holt, who was also a CIA man, did claim to have been the third tramp. If I am wrong about Hunt being the third tramp, it might be Chauncy Marvin Holt. There was work done with photography overlay that does indicate that this man might be the third tramp if it wasn't Hunt.

I see at least seven shots and at least three assassins. My theory has Oswald as one of the assassins, with one behind the wall on the knoll and the other behind the fence in the parking lot. There may have been as many as seven assassins with as many as ten shots, maybe more, I am not sure.

I've changed my beliefs about how the assassination occurred from what they were at one time. I used to believe that Oswald killed Kennedy and the knoll shots were secondary. I believed Oswald and the assassin behind the wall fired, almost simultaneously. The first shot missed the limousine, while the second, from the knoll, caught Kennedy in the throat. The third hit John Connally in his back. I could see that Kennedy was facing forward. The Warren Commission had concluded that JFK's throat wound was an exit wound. I could see right away that this did not work. He would have felt the pain at the point of entry. He probably would not have felt the exit wound at all.

The "magic bullet" was said to have been found on the stretcher which had carried Governor Connally. The fourth came from behind the fence in the parking lot, which caused the multiple bullet fragments which were dug out of Connally's wrist. There are bullets that explode on impact. They said the magic bullet was intact. That is why I believed the wrist damage to John Connally was a knoll shot. The fifth shot, which was fatal to the president, came from Oswald's gun. Now I am convinced there will probably be as many as six gunmen and as many as ten shots. In my earlier works, I did not mention the evidence of other bullet damage besides what was caused to the people in the car.

There was a bullet hole in the windshield of the car. It is quite clear that this bullet hole had been caused by a shot from the front. There were three bullet holes in the sign for the John Stennis Freeway. This sign was immediately removed after the assassination. There was a bullet taken out of a wall and another from a grassy patch. There was also a shot that hit the pavement behind the limousine, after the headshot occurred.

I have changed my mind about the technical evidence. I am now convinced that the fatal shot to the president's head came from behind the fence in the parking lot. In fact, by now I am sure that there were possibly two headshots in JFK, two back shots. There might have been a third wound in JFK's back and the throat wound. There is much that I agree with the conspiracy theorists about.

There was a wound in Kennedy's back. It was in the middle of his back, which was too far down for this bullet to have traveled upward and exited from his throat. This is probably what happened to Oswald's last shot if, in fact, the fatal shot came from the front. I believe now that there were shots fired from the Dal-Tex Building. This building was directly behind the motorcade. The autopsy photographs done on JFK do show two back wounds in Kennedy and that the photograph was tampered with. The doctors at Bethesda Naval Hospital mentioned a back wound, about an inch and a half deep that was close to the president's shoulder. I used to wonder why the doctors who had examined President Kennedy's body did not regard his back wounds to be fatal. Recently, I learned that JFK was wearing a back brace for support because he had a bad back.

That is why Jim Garrison and the others who support his views believe Oswald was actually framed. Perhaps, the success or failure of this operation was all that stood between world peace and nuclear war. The fate of the human race may have rested Oswald's marksmanship. Initially, they probably planned to just use Oswald. I don't see where it would have benefited the people behind this to have had Oswald framed. They knew that the birds were really going to fly if Oswald had missed. I am aware of the evidence the conspiracy theorists have brought forth which has convinced people that Oswald was not even a gunman at all. There is a lot here that does not add up. They may be right. However, the evidence might not all be credible.

The point I am getting at is if Oswald was framed, there would not have been the need for any other gunmen. Then, there would not have been any reason for a technical cover-up. Instead of three shots, there would have been just *one* shot and the president would have been dead.

This would have been Oswald's first kill. As far as we know, Oswald had never taken a human life before. It was indeed questionable whether or not he would really be able to kill the president. Oswald was a lousy shot, and he had a lousy old gun. It is because they did use Oswald as an assassin that they needed to have all these other gunmen there.

This is what caused all the conspiracy controversy to start up. Otherwise, the files would have been sealed and the book on this would have been closed in 1964. Without the technical controversy, Jim Garrison would not have been able to prosecute Clay Shaw.

Mark Lane would not have been able to write *Rush to Judgement*. Edward J. Epstein would not have been able to write *Inquest*. The hearings, which were held in the late seventies, would not have taken place. Again, it was all this technical controversy that got this investigation reopened in the 1970s. So much focus was being placed on the technical controversy that there was a time when I believed that the other shots were actually a mistake. However, I definitely know for sure that they were no mistake!

However, it was a mistake for them to have used Clay Shaw of New Orleans for this because of the problem with his personal life. I'm referring to the homosexual relationship between Clay Shaw and David Ferrie. This caused a security leak.

Oswald was psychologically capable of political assassination. He was a very unhappy, frustrated young man who had a lot of hostility in him. He had a gun, and he knew how to use it. Therefore, I cannot buy the idea that Oswald was framed.

By 1963, Oswald's mental condition was deteriorating. He really was getting to the point where he was becoming a threat to society. Up until the last year of his life, Lee Harvey Oswald was, for the most part, a lot of noise. He just liked to talk. He had a bad attitude about him, but he really was not dangerous.

However, by the spring of 1963, he purchased two guns. He went stalking a US Army general named John Walker in April of 1963. Then he fired on a United States general because he had quit the army to join the John Birch society. He was beating up Marina where before he would never hit her. She had to lock him in the bathroom to prevent him from shooting Richard Nixon. Then, he wrote the note to FBI Agent Hosty threatening to blow up the FBI office with two bombs.

So you can see where they had to do something with him to protect people, innocent people like Marina and her two babies. With the way he was getting, he could have come home one night and used that gun on Marina and those two kids and then turned the gun on himself. His mind was really going.

They had a man who would do this for them without being asked to and without being paid. All they had to do was feed him certain intelligence information which they knew would anger Oswald enough to make him decide of his own accord to kill the president. He was manipulated, in other words. Instead of planting false evidence in the sniper's nest, they simply planted information which they knew would anger Oswald enough to make him decide of his own accord to kill the president. He was manipulated, in other words. Instead of planting false evidence in the sniper's nest, they simply planted information with the sniper which they knew would cause him to react this way.

I did not believe that there was any evidence of the CIA/Mafia plots to assassinate Fidel Castro until the information surfaced during the Frank Church Hearings in 1973. A document was declassified in 2017. According to this document, Oswald did know that the CIA was trying to assassinate Castro prior to the JFK assassination. This newly released document said that Oswald was outraged when he read a newspaper article in which Fidel Castro was saying that the CIA had been trying to kill him.

I can only say that I now believe that this is the reason why Oswald got on a bus and went to New Orleans. This could be the reason why this Pro-Marxist Castro supporter managed to infiltrate the anti-Castro group. He wanted to find out if this was true. My guess is that these people in New Orleans made it clear to Oswald that it told him this, on purpose, knowing it would make him angry enough to want to kill Kennedy.

There was no reason for them to go through the trouble or take the unnecessary risks they'd have had to take in order to frame an innocent man. They just had to strike the match and light the fuse. The dynamite was already in his head. They just had to ignite it.

I titled my book *Probable Cause* because there was enough evidence to arrest some of these people by the late 1970s. However, I do not believe this is really going to be a criminal case. I am not asking anyone to take my word for anything. I am just trying to make people see the need for this case to be reopened.

Some of the ideas I express in this book are decades old. I began writing my ideas on this back in 1980, '81, '82, and

'83. After the Congressional and Senate Hearings on the JFK assassination, books like *Best Evidence, Conspiracy, The Plot to Kill the President*, etc. started coming out. When I read the books, which were published containing the evidence of conspiracy, I found that two names had been leaked during the Schweiker-Hart hearings in 1979.

At first, I didn't suspect that these two names, E. Howard Hunt and David Atlee Phillips, were dropped on purpose.

E. Howard Hunt wrote mystery books. I thought that David Atlee Phillips wrote the same kind of books Hunt wrote. The man I was thinking about turned out to be James Atlee Phillips. So far, nobody had stopped to think about these books!

During his lifetime, E. Howard hunt wrote and published eighty-eight books. Eighty-five of them were short spy thrillers, two autobiographies, and a documentary about the Bay of Pigs called *Give Us This Day*. His friend Phillips has written and published about thirty. I do not know whether or not you are familiar with their books, but in case you are not, I will tell you what their books are like and what they write about.

Howard Hunt's early books are something like the old Dashiell Hammett novels or the Raymond Chandler Marlowe Books, like *The Lady in the Lake* or *The Big Sleep*. Some of them remind me a lot of the Saint books by Leslie Charteris. His early espionage novels are something like the Graham Greene's old books such as *Our Man in Havana, This Gun for Hire, The Third Man,* or *Confidential Agent*. By the sixties, his style changed to become something like early Frederick Forsythe *The Day of the Jackal* or *The Odessa File.*

His books tend to lack character development. The emphasis is mainly on the plot, which is why they have fallen a little short of being best seller material. However, his books read like a roller-coaster ride where you cannot see the tracks. They are intensely suspenseful. He really does know how to write a real thriller.

The other man, David Atlee Phillips, had an older brother named James Atlee Phillips. He was a famous author of spy thriller books as well as an intelligence officer in the CIA. I admit I'd made the mistake of assuming that James Atlee Phillips and David Atlee Phillips were one and the same guy.

James Atlee Phillips was commonly called Jim Phillips. He wrote a series of books during the 1950s, '60s, and '70s. He used to publish his books under the pen name Phillip Atlee.

The twenty-six books written by Jim Phillips, a.k.a. Phillip Atlee, always had the word *contract* at the end of the title. This is why they became known as the Contract series. His books reminded me of the Nick Carter books, the Matt Helm books by Donald Hamilton, or the Executioner series by Don Pendleton.

After David Atlee Phillips retired from the CIA in 1975, he did write and publish five books of his own. His autobiography is called *Night Watch.* He wrote a documentary *The Great Texas Murder Trials*, a novel called *The Terror Brigade,* and *Careers in Secret*

Operations. His first published novel was called *The Carlos Contract.* The title of this book is what mislead me to assume that he had written all these other books about Joe Gall. I didn't suspect at the time that David Phillips had deliberately chosen to end the title of his first novel Contract so that people would think he had written all his brother's books!

Memories had come to me from when I was just a kid. Because of his close friendship with E. Howard Hunt and because of the similarity of their names, I just took it for granted that David Phillips was the Phillips Atlee who wrote all the successful novels from the 1950s to the early 70s. I never thought that there would have been another man working as an intelligence officer for the CIA around the same time who would have had the same middle and last name.

Both Phillips and Hunt worked together in Guatemala in 1954 and then later during the Bay of Pigs invasion in 1961. They both wrote about relationship in their own autobiographies. Hunt discussed their relationship in his book *Give Us This Day.*

You may be wondering where these books fit in with the Kennedy Conspiracy. Believe it or not, these books are the due to how they staged his assassination. I have both Hunt and Phillips on the motives, the methods by which the crime was committed, and the fact that there is significant evidence, which strongly indicates that they had the opportunity to commit the crime in this manner.

However, I do not see this as a crime that was committed but as an intelligence deception, which was brilliantly staged to look like a crime had been committed. That was the whole idea.

So that the whole world would be in such a state of shock because of the tragic events in Dallas, that hopefully, whoever was going to declare nuclear war on us might decide to back down and forget about it. They would wait then to see what the new leader was going to be like and what he was going to do.

If the conditions in the world which were leading to was improved with the change in the administration, then there wouldn't be any reason to have to go to war with the United States.

Now let me explain where these books fit in.

Anyone who writes mysteries knows that you cannot prosecute someone for murder using the power of suggestion. People are considered legally and morally responsible for their own actions. This means that no matter what you might say to someone, which may suggest the idea of murder, the intent to kill enters their own minds of their own accord, and they are considered solely responsible for their own behavior.

In addition, anyone who writes mysteries has to be able to understand people and their motives, especially when it comes to what motivates them to kill and commit murder. To a mystery writer, everyone is capable of murder . . . It is just a matter of having enough motive. Understanding people's motives for murder is very important in mystery writing.

The way they set their assassins off was to feed them certain intelligence information that they knew will anger them enough to make the kill whoever they want to out of the way.

The people they used for this were human time bombs, who were emotionally unstable misfits. These guys in the CIA just figured out what to say to these people that would make them, of their own accord, decide to kill someone they wanted to be killed. In other words, they would just apply a little psychology and let them do the rest.

For example, all Hunt had to tell Oswald is that Kennedy ordered Castro's assassination. Knowing Oswald's sympathies and where his loyalties lie and knowing his resentments, he deliberately fed Oswald information about all the espionage activity that was being committed against Castro and make it very clear to him that Kennedy was behind it.

Upon learning of this, he was so outraged that he, of his own accord, decided to try to kill the president. At that time in our history, very few people could have known that Kennedy had ordered Fidel Castro's assassination. Howard Hunt suggested this idea to Kennedy in 1961. We know by now that Kennedy eventually did order Castro assassinated and even involved the Mafia in these attempts, so who would have known this at the time . . . besides E. Howard Hunt?

All they had to tell Ruby is that Oswald was going to get away with it! The way Jack Ruby had been behaving would have drawn their attention to him, if they did not already know him. I personally believe that the decision to use Ruby to kill Oswald was made sometime after Oswald was already in custody for the murder of Officer Tippit. So far, I really cannot tell just where the murder of the cop fits in.

However, they probably told Ruby that because Oswald has never read his legal rights when he was arrested, he'd been held in custody for more than twenty-four hours without being appointed an attorney, and he'd made statements both to the police as well as to the public without consent of an attorney. This would have thrown his case out court.

Therefore, it is easy to figure out that this was Ruby's motive for killing Oswald. The nightclub owner who loved John F. Kennedy was not going to let the person who murdered his hero in cold blood get off free on a legal technicality.

So he made up his mind that he was not going to let him get away with it. He knew he had cancer and would be dead within a few short years, so he had nothing to lose by it. Perhaps now you see where these mystery books tie in with this and how these books are the clues to who the human minds are behind the Kennedy curse.

There is a ton of evidence linking Hunt and Phillips to this assassination and evidence which links Howard Hunt directly to Oswald. If I were to try to include all the evidence of E. Howard Hunt's involvement with the Kennedy assassination, we would have a book that wouldn't even fit on shelf. We would need a whole bookcase and maybe more. I believe that when you add my new evidence to the other evidence of Hunt's involvement, we had enough evidence to establish a probable cause for his arrest and for the arrest of many of the other people connected to this.

Yet I am sure that these people are not going to be guilty of any crime. At least not for this.

Just as the first publication of this book went to press, E. Howard Hunt passed away. At that time, I was unaware of the extensive confessions that E. Howard Hunt had given his son, Saint John Hunt.

In the fall of 2009, I went on the internet to see if any new information had come out which would support my theories. The first thing I came across was an article in a *Rolling Stone* magazine. It was titled "The Last Confessions of E. Howard Hunt." It surprised me that he had done a lot of talking during his last years. He had given his son, Saint John, a lot of information.

I contacted Saint John and began a correspondence with him via email. He had written a book about his relationship with his late father and the confessions that he'd extracted from him between 2003 and 2006. I bought the manuscript for his book *Bonds of Secrecy* and a DVD with the same title as the *Rolling Stones* article.

Saint John's story should have been front page news. Yet the press really played it down, practically blackballing it. I was surprised that he faced such an uphill battle with the book publishers and the news media. He had been on a program called *Inside Edition*, but other than that, the media really killed his story.

Anyhow, Saint John Hunt finally published his book by 2011, and it was released for sale by the end of 2012. Jesse Ventura, the host of the show *Conspiracy Theory* wrote the forward, which was not in the manuscript.

I strongly recommend reading this book. It should be a best seller. Saint John has proven that he has his late father's talent as a writer.

CHAPTER THREE
The "Bishop" controversy, Hunt's Libel Lawsuits, and Evidence of JFK's Own Involvement

Perhaps you already know about the Bishop Controversy, which was discussed in the book *Conspiracy* by Anthony Summers. I was sure, at one time, that E. Howard Hunt would be the man who was seen with Oswald using the name Maurice Bishop. In 1977, a man named Antonio Veciana testified that he saw a man with Oswald in August of 1963. This man, Veciana, was shot in the forehead when an attempt was made on his life for testifying about this. There was a controversy that arose during the Senate Intelligence Committee in 1979. (This committee was headed by Sen. Richard Schweiker and Sen. Gary Hart.) The controversy had to do with the true identity of a man named Maurice Bishop. The committee was led to the conclusion that David Atlee Phillips was Bishop. The conspiracy theorists believed that Phillips was Bishop. I thought they were wrong and that it would be Hunt.

This time the conspiracy theorists were correct. For many years Mr. Veciana would not speak of this. As of this writing, this man is still alive, and he has been talking. There are numerous videos on YouTube where Veciana makes it clear that David Atlee Phillips was the man he saw in Mexico City with Oswald. Victor Marchetti, in his spotlight article, said Hunt was to be "thrown to the wolves" during these hearings. He said they were going to leak just enough evidence so that Hunt would be caught.

Howard Hunt did use the cover name Bishop when he worked with David Atlee Phillips during the Bay of Pigs in 1961 and during the overthrow of the government of Guatemala in 1954. During these operations, David Phillips used the cover name Knight. They made much of this in their own books. This is why I believed Hunt would be Bishop and not David Phillips. I had just assumed that they were still using the same cover names they had used when they worked together on earlier operations.

According to Mr. Veciana, David Atlee Phillips also used the cover name Maurice Bishop when he worked on assassination attempts of the life of Fidel Castro. There is evidence that places David Phillips in Mexico City at the time of Oswald's visit. He was said to have been the station chief at the US Embassy in Mexico City. Also, when E. Howard Hunt gave his confessions to his son, Saint John, he said, "Phillips, for the most part, handled Oswald." So, both E. Howard Hunt and David Atlee Phillips had used the name Bishop undercover.

(This note is courtesy of Saint John Hunt. It is also public domain.).

Nov.8,1963

Dear Mr. Hunt,

*I would like information concerning my
position.*

*I am asking only for information. I am
suggesting that we discuss*

*the matter fully before any steps are taken
by me or anyone else.*

Thank You,

Lee Harvey Oswald

I did try to reach the Senate Intelligence Committee to inform them of this, but I could not get past the people who work in their offices. They just kept telling me that the hearings were over, the case was now closed, and the matter has been aside. The committee's attention is being devoted to more contemporary issues, so my theory kept coming back.

Hunt sued the Liberty Lobby for libel back in 1981 and won the case. He was awarded $650,000 in damages. I'd sent my theory to Liberty Lobby, along with the evidence I'd found to support my claims, but their legal department told me that they wouldn't be able to use my theory at their trial because the Kennedy case was not closed and therefore new evidence would not be admissible in their defense (I never got the woman's name).

The main point Mr. Marchetti was trying to make through the article did prove out, but the Senate ignored the evidence. E. Howard Hunt lost this case on appeal in 1985. Mark Lane defended Liberty Lobby, and he lost the $650,000 he was originally awarded and had to pay $25,000 in sanctions to Liberty Lobby for legal fees.

The Washington attorney Mark Lane wrote a book about the case called *Plausible Denial*. According to Mr. Lane, the main focus of this trial was about whether or not E. Howard Hunt was in Dallas on November 22, 1963. Apparently, the people who testified as Hunt's defense witnesses were all his immediate family members and CIA personnel. These witnesses were not considered credible since they were all people who would have had a reason to lie for him.

There is evidence that places E. Howard Hunt in Dallas on the day of Kennedy's death. Robert J. Groden has a whole gallery of photographs of Hunt in Dallas on November 22, 1963. They are, or at least were, available over the internet. Mr. Groden is famous for the work he has done with the photography of the assassination and has also made several documentary videos about it which are excellent.

There is also a photograph of Dorothy Hunt in Dallas on November 22, 1963. She is the woman with her hand over her mouth, watching her husband being released as one of the three tramps!

There is another evidence of E. Howard Hunt's involvement which I will discuss later in this book.

I want to make a point about the president's involvement in his own assassination plot. I made a point earlier in the book that the president was aware of the plot to kill him and that he went along with it voluntarily. This was not done without his knowledge and consent. I'm also sure that this new evidence which indicates that the vice president was aware of the plot in advance is also valid when I first started writing about this back in the 1980s.

The people who are behind this would have known enough to make the president order this himself. I am sure they fully discussed this with him beforehand and made him aware of the reason for why they had to do this. I am sure they have a legal document or a series of them and perhaps a film or a tape where he gave them his authorization to take him out. They actually convinced him to go along willingly to Dallas, where he deliberately left himself vulnerable to assassination so they would be able to kill him. Richard Helms was in a position where he had direct access to the president. I am sure he is the man who got the president to cooperate.

Richard Helms was the CIA's director of operations at the time of the Kennedy assassination. He also ran the MKUltra mind control program between 1953 and 1973. MKUltra ended in 1973 when President Nixon fired Helms. It is the responsibility of the director of operations to obtain the president's signature on an executive order for any operation—foreign or domestic.

The executive order is a paper that says, in Harry Truman's words, "The buck stops here." It means that the responsibility for an operation rests with him on his desk in the White House.

This gives the intelligence agencies the right to operate above the law. It gives them the right to circumvent the written laws which generally apply to a situation.

It gives them the right to do things in espionage, which normally would carry a criminal charge and makes them immune from criminal prosecution. There are things the intelligence community has to do at times to protect the safety of the nation, which would be prosecutable as criminal offenses. The executive order makes them immune from prosecution.

When I first wrote this theory, I believed there would be just one document that the president would have signed. Now I believe there will be a series of executive orders which were signed by JFK. Then, there would have been other papers signed by LBJ after the assassination and documents signed by other people in key government positions as well. I believe that the name of this kind of cover is called a blanket cover because it spreads out like a blanket.

I was thinking that the CIA officers made JFK sign the same documents that Barack Obama signed for the assassination of Bin Laden in Pakistan. I believe that the title of the legal statute this comes under is called government-sponsored targeted killing.

My theory has drawn much criticism from people in the JFK assassination community because I brought forth evidence of the president's own involvement in this. I agree wholeheartedly with the conspiracy theorists about the fact that there is a case here. However, I am trying to explain to people the reason why they have not been able to get a criminal prosecution on this.

I know a lot of people may find this hard to believe, but I am sure that the late Dick Helms made the late president sign the executive orders for this executive action himself. This would make it a legitimate covert intelligence operation of the United States Government. It really was a covert operation. It is not that the government is obstructing justice by helping criminals to evade prosecution for a wrongdoing, as alleged by Jim Garrison. I would say it was really a right doing that was made to look like a wrongdoing for a reason. The reason I am convinced that it was Helms is because of the position he was in at the time. It is also because of what I know about him and about the other men who were there at the time. I believe there were other men in the room when these documents were signed. By now, they are all dead.

I believe there were intelligence reports that were put on the desks of these CIA executives. I can only say that I believe that what was written in those reports are what sealed Kennedy's doom. It was nothing personal or political that moved these men to take this action. I did not mention these intelligence reports in any previous versions of this book because I have never seen them. People would want me to produce proof in writing that these documents exist. Of course, I have no written proof. I believe these documents do exist, but at this time I am sure they are still classified.

If it had not been for the president's cooperation, the assassination would have failed.

The assassination is not the result of a criminal conspiracy but a legitimate covert intelligence operation of the United States government. It was perpetrated from within the United States government and even authorized by the late president himself.

This was done to maintain world peace, to protect our national safety and security. They also had to preserve the credibility of the United States government and to preserve the president's image in the minds of the American people. They wanted him to be remembered as the man they had come to know and love as their president. This way people would remember the beauty of the photogenic First Family and the elegance, the pomp, and circumstance of the Camelot Court. They would remember JFK as the scholarly aristocrat who had a stature as a statesman and so on.

Only the good things would be remembered. Only the positive accomplishments of his administration would be emphasized, his famous speeches, familiar quotations, etc.

In other words, they wanted him to be remembered as the man who accompanied Mrs. Kennedy to Dallas.

On November 22, 1963, JFK was joking with reporters, saying, "They once said I would always be remembered as the man who accompanied Mrs. Kennedy to Paris. Now, I will always be remembered as the man who accompanied Mrs. Kennedy to Dallas." This was filmed and shown on television. When he was at the Texas Hotel in Fort Worth, he was quoted as having said, "Last night would have been a hell of a night to assassinate the president."

The controversy surrounding this remark is whether he said it in the evening of November 21 or in the morning of the twenty-second. I believe this is in the Warren Report. He was talking publicly when he made these comments.

Anyhow, the image of JFK and Jackie in the death car would be embedded in the psyche of the American public.

Yet they would have dealt with the danger. Our government would survive, and innocent people here in the United States and elsewhere in the world would remain safe.

The ugliness, they hoped, would remain sealed off and hidden away from the American public. They hoped it would remain hidden anyhow—buried deep in those files, which would remain classified until, well, into this present century.

JFK ignored all the warnings not to go to Dallas. He was told he was riding into hostile territory and that it was very likely an attempt would be made on his life. The evangelist Billy Graham warned him about the danger of making this trip. Kennedy responded by quoting the Bible. He said, "What does it profit a man to gain the world if only to lose his soul?"

It shows that his own life at this point meant nothing. He was a man who was ready to die.

The limousine picked up John and Nelly Connally first. There was an off-white plastic bubble top over the car, with four secret service agents in place riding on the rear bumper of the car. When the death car named Lancer arrived at Love Field, the bubbletop was still in place over the car.

When JFK and Jackie disembarked from Air Force One, JFK gave the order to remove the plastic bubbletop and gave the order to secret service agents were to ride on the back of the car. My source here is *Death of a President* by William Manchester. There is a film which is now available on YouTube showing the bubbletop coming off Lancer at Love Field.

The conspiracy theorists also make much of the formation of the police motorcycles in the motorcade. There are usually two police motorcycles that run in front of the president's limousine. They claim that the motorcycle policemen were ordered by the Secret Service to ride behind the Lancer death car instead of in front of it. According to both the Warren Report and the Secret Service agents who were there, this was arranged by the president as well.

There is also a film showing JFK ordering the Secret Service agents not to ride on the tail end of the car. This is also available on YouTube. Conspiracy theorists insist that the head of the Secret Service gave this order. However, if you watch this video closely, you will see that the body language clearly shows that the order came from JFK.

Gerald Blaine's book *The Kennedy Detail* is an excellent source for the evidence that JFK kept trying to keep the Secret Service off the car. He did this in Tampa, as well as in Miami, and in Dallas. There is another book by Vince Palamara which counters and conflicts with this called

Survivor's Guilt. It seems there is great controversy among these Secret Service men as to who ordered these security precautions removed.

There is other evidence of JFK's own involvement. An audio tape, declassified in the summer of 2012, recorded him saying, "Monday is going to be a bad day." How could he have known that the coming Monday would be the day of his funeral?

Also, Jackie was the only woman in the motorcade to be presented with a bouquet of red roses. All the other women were given yellow roses. She even commented about this. I remember reading somewhere that JFK changed the color of roses for Jackie from yellow to red at the last minute. I am not sure of my sources for this, but this does indicate that he was involved.

Another fact was made public in the fall of 2011. Caroline Kennedy Schlossberg released statements that Jackie Kennedy gave to a man named James Schlesinger shortly after the assassination.

According to what Jackie told this man, she told JFK, "Should it come down to either a nuclear war or your assassination, I don't want to be protected. I don't want to be hidden away. I want to be right there with you by your side. I love you so much, Jack. I want to die with you."

I know that legally this is going to be considered hearsay evidence. It is just what one person long dead said to another person long dead that they said to someone who was dead even longer. However, if this true, it accounts for why Jackie was in the position she was placed in that day. It's probably because she asked to be.

Who would have known that but JFK?

So there is evidence that indicates that JFK was not a victim of a crime but a willing participant in this massive deception.

CHAPTER FOUR
More Evidence to Support My Case

I do agree with one thing that Garrison said in the movie *JFK*. He said there were some mob figures involved with this at the lower levels of the assassination but not at the top. At the top is a government operation all the way! I believe that one reason for why the government allowed these Mafia men to play a role in this is so that if any controversy ever started up about it, they would have a scapegoat. People would think, as some do now, that Kennedy's assassination was a mob hit to throw people off the real reason for this.

When I first found out about this massive conspiracy and cover-up of enormous proportions, involving hundreds of people at the highest levels of the United States government, the hundreds of files containing thousands of documents linking all aspects of United States Intelligence with this, the Mafia, the Dallas Police Department, LBJ, etc., I knew that the problem was going to turn out to be with the president.

From this, I found myself asking some very serious questions about the president's personal moral character, his personality, and his state of mental health. So I started investigating him! Instead of runaway intelligence community, I strongly suspected right from the beginning that what the intelligence community had on its hands was a very sick president!

I figured that the most admired and respected president the country ever had in its history would turn out to be the closet Caligula we had in the White House, whom they absolutely had to assassinate or else we were going to be hit with nukes because of all the high crimes and barbaric acts of terrorism he was ordering to be carried out all over the world from that office. They had to prove to the Soviets that Americans want peace and will stop at nothing to see that it's maintained!

What I am saying is that the CIA felt they had no choice but to kill President John F. Kennedy. He was America's favorite president, whom the whole world admired. Yet our own intelligence had to kill him in a very violent, public way or everyone in the world was going to die in the most horrible ways imaginable.

Back in 1941, after the Pearl Harbor attack, the United States government vowed—never again! Never again would America be attacked by a foreign power. This JFK assassination shows us just how far the United States government was willing to go in order to keep this promise to the American people.

On September 11, 2001, the United States was attacked. However, the attack was launched by an international criminal terrorist organization. However, the 9/11 attacks were a criminal act, which is not the same thing as an act of war declared by a foreign government.

The arms race with the Soviet Union has been defeated and the war we have always dreaded never came. However, while Japan has its Hiroshima Memorial, we here in the United States have our Kennedy Grave, where the eternal flames continually burn. Both stand as monuments to the terror of nuclear weapons and to the tragedies that have already come about because of their existence!

I hope that the outcome of the "Story That Won't Go Away" will end up teaching Americans everywhere a lesson they'll never forget!

When I first began writing this book, most of the men who planned this assassination were still alive. However, there are some people living today who have knowledge of these events. Action needs to be taken soon if we want to learn the whole truth.

My objective is to get them to talk—to tell us the truth themselves while they are still living. I want them to be there when these files and documents are examined so they will be able to answer whatever questions may arise.

I was angry about the reason they gave for this in the Oliver Stone movie. This man Helms was personally opposed to our military involvement in Vietnam. From what this man has said himself, he certainly would not want our troops to be forced to fight in Vietnam for ten more years.

The agency executives were never Hawk on Nam. The agency tried for years to keep us out of Vietnam because their analysts were telling them that use of force would not be in our best interests. All throughout the Vietnam War, Richard Helms and most of the agency executives voiced their opposition to our military involvement there and were trying to get us out.

The conspiracy authors and theorists like Jim Garrison, Mark Lane, Anthony Summers, Oliver Stone, etc. all see the agency executives of that era as right-wing radicals, fanatics, and extremists. They consider JFK a peace-loving liberal, who was in the way of a right-wing plot to escalate the Vietnam War so people in the intelligence community and the military hardware industry could make money.

Richard Helms would have used espionage tactics only to keep the South Vietnamese government in power. If agency efforts had failed, he would have thrown a lot of support to other countries in the surrounding region to try to protect them.

He had voiced the opinion that Vietnam should have been an agency war, not military. In other words, he believed this war should have been fought with covert aid and clandestine operations for the most part, not with troops on the ground. He would have supplied the South Vietnamese and helped to train their troops, but that is as far as he would have gone. In *Conspiracy* by Anthony Summers, it was suggested that this was done so they could get Castro because Kennedy wouldn't do enough to help them.

Richard Helms was almost fired from the CIA twice for trying to stop the Bay of Pigs invasion. His position on Cuba at the time was that our policy toward Cuba should be defensive only. He was opposed to any offensive strategy being used there whatsoever. He believed Castro should have been kept under very close surveillance but not forcefully overthrown or killed. Richard Helms was also opposed to the nuclear arms race believing it would eventually be the ruination of both the US and the USSR. Even if no nuclear was ever fought, the competition to build up stockpiles of these weapons would result in economic ruin for both countries. This was his opinion at the time, and he was right.

I have been studying these men, learning as much as I can about their beliefs, their careers, and their true personalities. Jim Garrison did not think to do this. He was too emotionally reactionary and too politically prejudiced to be able to analyze intelligent information objectively in order to form and draw responsible conclusions without distorting it. He knew where to find this kind of information, but he did not know how to interpret it right because his mind was not clear.

Don't get me wrong, the conspiracy theorists and independent researchers did a remarkable job. They had great courage to take it on themselves to investigate this matter. If it hadn't been for their efforts, the vast majority of people would still believe the Warren Report. Today, we can conclusively prove that our government did not tell us the truth about how and why this president died.

However, they did not really take the time to really study the people whom their investigations led to. Believe me, I am not saying this with any disrespect toward the conspiracy theorists. They are all very brilliant, remarkable human beings. It is just that they are blind as bats when it comes to their ability to read and understand people from a distance.

The criminal conspiracy theorists just remembered JFK as the politician. They still saw and still just tend to see his image, his persona! Then, they just put politics on the people they connected to this assassination. They based their theories on their prejudices, without really trying to understand the people themselves.

Richard Helms was exceptionally rational. He had a very clear and quiet mind and a very charming, gracious, elegant manner. He could read people very clearly, up front as well as from a distance. He was very good when it came to working with people. He was also very deceptive. I would say that he could have sold ice boxes to Eskimos. He could steal the eyes out of someone's head and then convince them that it was dark outside.

He could read about someone in a file which had been put together by a CIA analyst and pull the thoughts out of their head from all the way over on the other side of the world. He was extremely sensitive and perceptive to the point where I would say he was almost psychic, especially when it came to foreign affairs and intelligence matters.

This man was very secretive, evasive, elusive, and like I said, deceptive. He would always lie to just about everyone. For the most part, he would be truthful to the people who worked for him, but then he would only tell them what they needed to know to carry out a specific operation and that would be it! He would not even talk to them very much.

While this man believed very much in secrecy, he did have outstanding character, and he was very mature, stable, and responsible.

I thought this man knew more about the JFK assassination than anyone else. At least I felt he would have been the most qualified to account for the facts to the people. He would have known the answers to questions that would not have been found in the files and documents alone.

Sadly, Richard Helms passed away on October 21 of 2002 at age eighty-nine. He died from multiple myeloma, a cancer of the muscles and nerves.

This was the man whom I believe knew all the answers to the questions about this assassination. He knew the answers to questions that will not be found in the files and could answer whatever questions might pertain to the files and documents themselves. I was hoping that he would have lived.

The other man, E. Howard Hunt, the Watergate burglar, was more of an author than an espionage man. He reached the position of political action office at the time of the Bay of Pigs, but from there, he just seemed to fail. He was not fired from the CIA, but he was fired from every job he had ever held at the agency until he retired of his own free will in 1970. I think this man was basically a good man, but eventually he was driven to insanity by his own emotions. He had a career in espionage which spanned over thirty years, but I believe he had an author's personality. Due to his highly creative nature, he was just too sensitive to be able to handle this dark, clandestine espionage.

He was a very sick man, mentally by the early seventies. He really suffered a serious nervous breakdown. It was not this man's nature to be corrupt, but he was completely off the deep end at the time of the Watergate scandal. His books are very well-written. He had a very, very beautiful literary style. His knowledge and command of the English language was out of this world. His books almost always had a positive resolution, which is sign that basically, he was a positive person himself.

He just could not handle espionage psychologically. His personality was more like an Ernest Hemingway, F. Scott Fitzgerald, or Dashiell Hammett. He was not the cloak-and-dagger man that we see in his old boss Dick Helms. He was also writing about dark stuff in his novels. I really do believe that eventually it all caught up with him and drove him to insanity. Some of the people who were involved with the Watergate scandal may have been mentally and emotionally ill because of things they knew or had to do for the United States government.

Anyway, I want you to know Richard Helms and I had a common hobby. We both read and collected E. Howard Hunt's books. When I read *The Man Who Kept the Secrets*, Richard Helms's biography by Thomas Powers, I really freaked out when I got to the part about Hunt's books.

Richard Helms was reading and collecting Hunt's novels ever since 1956. Up until 1973, Hunt had never published his books in his own name. He used about four different pen names.

However, Helms, used to his books, would keep extra copies on his desk in his office and would hand them out to people who came in. My source for this fact in the book is in *The Man Who Kept the Secrets* by Thomas Powers, 1979.

In 1973, at the height of the Watergate scandal, E. Howard Hunt asked Richard Helms, who was then DCI, if he could publish his books in his own name. Helms said, "By all means I don't care what you do with your books." Helms was very angry and upset at the time because he was going to be fired by Richard Nixon for refusing to cover up for the Watergate crimes. I believe he made a little mistake because he was upset.

There is other evidence of E. Howard Hunt's involvement in the Kennedy assassination. During the Watergate scandal, there were things President Richard Nixon said, which were recorded on tapes. He said this involved Hunt and these Cubans and this whole Bay of Pigs thing. At another time, Nixon stated, "This Hunt, he knows things."

As I mentioned earlier, there is photographic evidence of Howard Hunt in Dallas on November 22, 1963, especially the picture taken of him as one of the three tramps who were arrested by the railroad tracks. (The photographer Robert J. Gordon has many other pictures besides this one.) His alibis failed in court. There are many discrepancies in his own testimony.

Also, the main target of the Watergate Hotel break-in and burglary was a man named Lawrence F. O'Brian. He is deceased. There is a Kennedy connection here, as well as a connection to both Kennedy assassinations. This man was JFK's campaign manager and later became Robert Kennedy's campaign manager. He was with JFK in Dallas when he was assassinated.

What did the Nixon administration hope to learn from illegally bugging this man's office? So far, we don't know; it's a question that pertains to the Watergate Scandal that has never been answered.

Also, when Deep Throat was talking to Bob Woodward (a reporter for the *Washington Post*), he said that Watergate is not about politics, it's operational, meaning CIA operations. We now know that Deep Throat is a man named Mort Felt who worked for the FBI.

According to the confessions Hunt gave his son, the men known as the Plumbers were after photographs of Hunt and other CIA personnel in Dallas on November 22, 1963. These pictures were made public after the Watergate scandal.

The third man, David Phillips, is a much harder man to get to know than Hunt and Helms. He managed to stay out of the scandals that broke out here in the seventies, so he has remained more of an obscure figure than the other two. All I could find about this man were his own books. It was difficult to find anything about this man's personality. However, there is much more information available about him over the internet than there was at one time.

There is much to be found about his education and his career. I was surprised to learn how liberal this man was. The more I studied him, the more I kept thinking that this man, David Atlee Phillips, is a lot like Richard Helms. Then I remembered back in 1954, during the Guatemala Operation, E. Howard Hunt gave him the nickname Knight because he reminded him of Richard Helms.

David Phillips also gave his confessions to his nephew, Shawn Phillips, the day before he died. Shawn is the only son of James Atlee Phillips, the man who wrote the Contract books using the pen name Phillip Atlee.

I don't know if anyone else was present when David Phillips spoke about his involvement in the JFK assassination. It was on July 6 of 1988—the day before he died.

Shawn told me about there was some bad blood between these two brothers because of David Phillips having been involved with the Kennedy assassination. James Phillips was also angry with his brother David for the fact that when David published his first novel, he called it *The Carlos Contract*. He did this deliberately so that people like me would think that he had written all his brother's books! I was only a child in grade school and junior high when I was reading these Contract books. The memories came back to me from a long, long time ago.

In the end, Lee Harvey Oswald will be vindicated of any criminal offense for the role he played in the Kennedy assassination. Jack Ruby, who was convicted of murder, will also have his criminal record erased. If Jim Garrison had managed to convict Clay Shaw, the man would have spent the rest of his life in jail, but eventually, his name would have been cleared.

There are a lot of people who find it difficult, if not impossible, to accept the idea that JFK authorized his own assassination and cooperated with his senior intelligence officers in a plot to have him assassinated. However, there is evidence that he was also involved, and the conspiracy theorists are so in denial of it. They are just blocking it out.

However, there were some factors that had in their favor, which would not have been present if they had been dealing with anyone else.

JFK was terminally ill with Addison's disease. He was also suffering from terrible pain, especially in his back. We now know that he was taking drugs. Some of them were legally prescribed by doctors, yet others were recreational drugs. Some of these drugs, like LSD, are known to make people susceptible to persuasion.

When people are terminally ill and in great pain, the idea of death becomes more acceptable to them. People have signed legal documents giving other people their permission to end their lives when these were their circumstances. They get to the point when they really want to die—to end their suffering. This is why the idea of doctor-assisted suicide is so controversial.

He did dread nuclear war. We know that this weighed very heavily on his mind throughout his administration. So the idea that his senior intelligence officers were able to obtain a direct presidential executive order from him for this is not at all far-fetched.

Morally, however, American society is responsible for it. There are failures in our government policies, both foreign as well as domestic that are responsible for this. It was also caused by social, psychological, and cultural problems that exist among the people of the United States.

It was also an intelligence failure that John F. Kennedy and his brother reached the positions they would attain in our government. If intelligence had reacted sooner, these tragedies would have been prevented.

I saw this man, Richard McGarrah Helms, on television occasionally, but I have read quite extensively about him in books. While I never met the man personally, I get the impression that his personality was somewhat like the fictional character Jim Phelps, whom Peter Graves portrayed on *Mission Impossible*.

He also reminds me of Mr. Clark of the Tom Clancy novels, especially when it comes to his moral reasoning. He also reminds me of Control from *The Spy Who Came in from the Cold* by John Le Carré. He was a real clandestine operations man who was exceptionally competent. He knew exactly what he was doing when it came to running operations and handling people. He seemed to have a talent for diplomacy as well as for the "dark stuff."

He had a gracious, elegant, charming manner about him. In his obituary, former Director of Central Intelligence George Tenet said that Helms had a clear mind and elegant style. George Tenet knew Richard Helms very well, personally. Helms helped train George Tenet and was also his advisor. George Tenet's perception of Richard Helms is very similar to my own when he knew him well, and I had never even met him.

In some of the earlier versions of this book, I said that Richard Helms never wrote any books himself, even though he was more than qualified to do so. However, there are letters and memos he had written which have been published in books written by other people. From his own statements, quotations, and things he has written and from things other people have said about him who knew him, I can't see where the late Jim Garrison (and the others who support his views) ever got the idea that this man Helms was a right-wing radical, a fanatic, and an extremist. He did eventually write his autobiography just before his death called *A Life in Intelligence*.

CHAPTER FIVE
My Efforts to Expose This

I wrote to Jim Garrison about this. He did have a chance to read this just before his death. I saw the Oliver Stone film. Then I read Jim Garrison's book *On the Trials of the Assassins*. Then I sent him a letter containing this same information. It took six months for it to reach him, since it had to go through other people to get to him.

I mailed my theory off in April of 1992.

It finally reached him by early October of that year. It was not in the form of a book yet. However, my information was presented well enough to get my ideas and theories across to him.

I sent it to his office at the Louisiana State Court of Appeals, in New Orleans, where he had been working as a judge. I did not know that he had resigned a month earlier, in March of 1992, due to ill health.

However, I kept calling his office to try to find out if he had received my package. An unidentified female voice kept telling me, "No, no, he has not yet received it. We have it here. It has not yet been given to him. He's very, very sick."

I would ask at times what was wrong with him. They would tell me that they were not at liberty to disclose the nature of his illness. Sometimes they would say they could not release any details of his condition to the public.

One day, in early November of 1992, I called his office again. This time the woman's voice said, "Yes, yes, he got it, and yes, it was read."

I asked her what was his reaction to it.

Her answer was "I don't know, he's dead."

I feel very badly about what happened to the late Jim Garrison. I was left wondering if my ideas had affected him like that. The people in his office kept telling me that he was very sick, but they never told me that it was his heart! I later learned that he had cancer. By now I know that I did not kill Jim Garrison.

I just wanted the people who were close to him know that I just wanted him to come to have a more realistic understanding of this assassination.

He was telling people that the people behind JFK's assassination were criminals at large who were guilty of a terrible wrongdoing for which they were never prosecuted. He believed this was an obstruction of justice on behalf of the United States government. He saw this as a criminal conspiracy within the government that the government had condoned. I wanted him to understand that it's not that, but something else . . .

So it seems poor Judge Garrison ended up becoming another mysterious death associated with the Kennedy Assassination. When I watched the Oliver Stone movie with Kevin Costner in the role of Jim Garrison, I could see that he was too emotionally reactive and too politically prejudiced to be able to analyze intelligence information without distorting it. He was actually paranoid. This seems to be a problem that all the conspiracy theorists seem to have.

I had only the sincerest intentions. I wanted to make him understand that there is a purpose for clandestine operations. Clandestine espionage is an essential aspect of our civil defense and plays just as important a role in maintaining our national safety as the military does.

There are times when intelligence has to create illusions which may deceive us in order to protect us from dangers that are real. When this is done, it's not the same thing as a crime.

People have written many books claiming that they know who really murdered JFK. I tried to convince Jim Garrison of the fact that nobody murdered the president. A lot of people were super mad at me when I said this. However, I have come to the conclusion that he is going to be "targeted killed" rather than murdered legally.

This was a black operation, which involved going above the law and required a government cover, but that does not mean there was a criminal conspiracy within the government, which the government condoned.

I thought this would help restore his faith in the United States government and in the integrity of the United States Intelligence.

Despite all the scandals and notoriety, I want to voice some strong words of praise for the men and women of the United States Intelligence. These people have done a remarkable job throughout the twentieth century keeping Americans safe and helping others elsewhere in the world to overcome oppression so they might come to have instilled in them our Democratic values.

We owe these people our lives; nevertheless, they owe the nation the truth by now about this Kennedy Operation.

When this book was first published as *Deception in Dallas*, Mr. Helms was still alive. I was afraid that when this man died, the truth about the JFK plot would be lost forever.

He also possessed a vast wealth of knowledge and experience pertaining to so many other things he'd seen and had been involved with. It is only because fate placed this man in the position he was in at the time that we were safe during the Cold War years. He is the only reason why we have managed to survive to see this new millennium.

This man witnessed a great deal of history and had a great deal to do with the making of American history during the twentieth century. I was hoping that the American people might have had a chance to really get to know the late Richard McGarrah Helms while he was still alive.

He was truly a remarkable man.

However, I did manage to make contact with a man who did know Richard Helms. In fact, he worked for him as his aid at the CIA.

Victor Marchetti, the author of the Spotlight article, read my book in its first publication. In August of 2004, I called him on the phone and asked him right out what he thought of it.

Mr. Marchetti told me, "It's the first book I have ever read on this subject that I would call loving, but it's truly a loving book." While I had Mr. Marchetti on the phone, I asked him if he would give me permission to republish his Spotlight article in my book. I want my readers to be able to read this. However, he flatly refused. At least I had a chance to ask him.

David Lifton, the author of the famous book *Best Evidence*, sent me a person response to my theory. He claims that the body of the president was altered while in flight from Dallas to Washington, DC. I agree that the evidence he found to support his position. It is indeed compelling. I believe that they did this, but also did a lot of other things as well to attempt to cover up for the damage caused by the other shots.

He is a die-hard criminal conspiracy theorist and swears that Oswald was framed with planted evidence. I did not want to use anything in this book that would be on the negative side, but on the other hand, I would like my readers to be informed of the opposition I am up against. My theory is competing against both the Warren Report and its supporters as well as having heterodoxies (dissenting opinions) with criminal conspiracy theories.

This is the letter I received from David Lifton dated November 4 of 2002.

> David Lifton
> 11500 W. Olympic Blvd., Suite 400
> Los Angeles CA 90064
> (310) 445-2399; Fax: (310) 445-2301
> Email: dlifton@earthlink.net
>
> Dear Robin Haines:
>
> I always wonder what drives different people who get interested in the JFDK case. I received your book. The cover is pretty. You obviously can string sentences together in an intelligible form, but when it comes to the ideas expressed I cannot accept 98% of it.
>
> The principal kernel of truth you have is that JFK was playing fast and loose with women. Yes, that's true (and to some, perhaps shocking). Then you speculate on what might have been the consequence. Here is where you veer off into outer space. In my opinion, you build a multi-level castle, that goes to the stratosphere. Most the ideas you set forth – which are actually just your own conjectures – have no basis in the record. The major theses you propose are not just improbable, they are ridiculous.

For your information: JFK was worried about a nuclear war. It dominated his thinking. It's because JFK and his instructions to Amb. Harriman that he have the nuclear test ban treaty. Reach Hugh Syndey's book, written and published prior to Dallas, if you want to get a valid assessment of JFK. Also, Richard Reeves, published in the last few years. That stuff is real, written by writers, who knew him personally, or are dealing with archival materials.

The notion that JFK's playing around invited a nuclear strike is straight out of your imagination, not rooted in reality. (Again, see these authors, or even Seymour Hersh on that score). Lee Oswald was not pro-Castro; he just appeared that way.

The shots that hit Kennedy struck from the front (See Best Evidence) That's why the body was altered, which is what my book is all about.

If the body was altered (to make it appear that LHO did shoot JFK), then obviously, from that it follows that LHO did NOT shoot JFK. Otherwise, why the necessity to alter the body? (So how can you say you agree with my work, and talk about the body being altered on the airplane, and then have Oswald as the shooter? (More inconsistencies. More lack of logic)

Richard Helms, in my opinion, was not involved, before the fact, in any plot to remove JFK from office. If you had reached him before he died, and if he had a sense of humor, he might have laughed at most of the ideas put forth in your book, but, more likely, it probably would have distressed him. And, if you elicited that ("distressed") response, you probably then would have mistakenly interpreted as indicating his guilt)

Comparisons between JFK and Hussein are absurd. Total nonsense.

Oswald was not "unhappy and frustrated" (p 48) Unaware that he was being set up, he was looking forward to the future, to being the father of two children, and to getting on with his life. There are lots of indications of this.

Apparently, you are unaware of them.

I could go on. It's as if you decided to do a weird shuffle with the facts of this case, and what you have come up with is something akin to a Jackson Pollak painting. It's a reflection of your own projections, conjectures.

Again, I do not understand why someone would take the time you apparently did to put all of this together, and yet be so off the mark. Given the major role your own personal conjectures and suspicions have played in assembling this montage (which clearly diverges from many well known facts), perhaps a more accurate subtitle would be— An Irrational Explanation . . . of the JFK Plot.

You asked me, so I'm telling you what I think.

Sincerely,
David Lifton

David Lifton just seems to see JFK's "woman problem" as his only problem. If a man is "playing it fast and loose with women," as Mr. Lifton put it, he is going to have other problems besides. If he had studied the whole person instead of just seeing the tip of the iceberg, he would know that his problem with women was just a red flag flying high, which should have indicated that JFK had a lot of serious problems that would be a major national security threat in the White House.

The conspiracy theorists, like Mr. Lifton, do not read or study their people at all whom their evidence pertains to. As you can see, from Mr. Lifton's letter to me, he is blindsided to everything that was really on with JFK. He just sees a sexual problem with women. By the time symptoms manifest in the kind of behaviors JFK was known to engage in, there are going to be a whole lot of problems below the waterline. It is what lies below the waterline that the ship is going to hit, and that is what is going to sink it.

I also was able to reach the famous newswoman Cokie Roberts. She read this before it was made into a book. She has always been interested in the JFK assassination.

Her late father, Congressman Hale Boggs, served on the Warren Commission. His plane disappeared over Alaska in 1967, and for this reason, he has been considered one of the mysterious deaths associated with the JFK plot.

She did give me a personal reply to my theory. Her comment was simply, "You could easily have followed in your late mother's footsteps as a journalist." I didn't think so. However, I considered this a great compliment coming from someone like her.

There is one more thing that I do want to say before I end this book. That is, I do not approve of the way the Kennedy Assassination was staged. I do not believe that they should have gunned him down in an open car that was carrying other passengers or in a parade where innocent people had gathered to see him. As it is, a governor was seriously injured and almost died. A man named James Tague was hit by a chip of pavement which hurt him in the throat. Later that day, a police officer named Tippet was killed. These were civilian casualties that could have been and should have been prevented. I did not get into the death of the police officer Tippet in this book. I am aware of all the controversy that surrounds that incident, but I am not sure exactly how it happened.

Apparently, other people were brought in on this who had absolutely no business being involved with an operation of this nature. This helped the cover to fail on this operation prematurely and cost a lot of these people their lives.

CHAPTER 6
My Phone Conversation with Buell Wesley Frazier

In mid-December of 2018, I had a two-hour conversation on the phone with Buell Wesley Frazier. I learned a great deal from him. He is the man who drove Oswald to work on the morning of the assassination. A lot of people believe that Ruth Paine found Lee Harvey Oswald the job at the Texas Book Depository. It was Mr. Frazier who told Mrs. Paine about the job. Buell Frazier was only nineteen years old at the time. He knew the Oswald family were living in Mrs. Paine's house in Irving Texas. He was living with his sister and her husband a few doors down the street. He was sleeping on their couch, so he was actually homeless himself.

I believe that if young Mr. Oswald ever had a true friend, it was Buell Wesley Frazier. He really is a very kind, caring Christian gentleman who was just trying to help. Then these tragic events took place on November 22, 1963, and he was dragged into a mess.

Mr. Frazier was the first person to cast doubt on Oswald's guilt. He always has expressed the position that the brown paper package that Oswald carried in the back of his 1953 Chevy was too small to have carried the gun that was said to have been the WWI-era Mannlicher-Carcano that was supposed to have been the weapon he used to kill Kennedy with. Even if the gun had been broken down, it would not have fit into the package that Oswald carried in his car that fateful morning.

In some of my earlier works, I had said this Doorway Man would be an Oswald impostor but not Oswald himself. Buell Frazier was standing on the top platform of the entrance of the book depository. He made it quite clear to me that Billy Lovelady was the Doorway Man. The so-called "Prayer Man" was not Oswald either. There were thirteen people who were out on the steps of the book depository while the assassination was going down. If Oswald had been out there with them, they would have gone down to the police department and made it clear that they had the wrong man. They would have said, "Pardon us, Captain Fritz and Deputy Craig, but you have arrested the wrong man. We do not know if he killed Officer Tippet or not because he left the building after the assassination, but he did not kill Kennedy because he was standing outside the building with us."

Mr. Frazier told me on the phone that Oswald left through the rear of the building. He said when Oswald arrived at work, he took off his grey Eisenhower jacket and took the shirt off that he was wearing. He hung his shirt on a hook and then hung his Eisenhower jacket on the hook over the shirt. He said that Oswald was just wearing a plain white T-shirt while he was working that morning. Buell

Frazier said when Oswald was about to leave, he watched him put his shirt back on and then he put his Eisenhower jacket on. He saw Oswald exit the building. He said he went down the steps of the loading platform in the rear of the building.

There are three other accounts of how Oswald left the book depository after the assassination. The most famous story about Oswald leaving the book depository was told by the famous television journalist Robert McNeil. When McNeil walked into the lobby immediately after the assassination, he encountered a young man in a brown shirt with the sleeves pushed up. He asked this man if there was a phone he could use. The young man pointed to some payphones and said, "Over there." However, Robert McNeil was not the first person who claimed to have encountered Oswald in the lobby immediately after the assassination. A man by the name of Pierce Allman actually entered the lobby of the book depository before Robert McNeil.

He was the program director for WFAA radio in Dallas at the time. Mr. Allman also claimed to have encountered this thin dark-haired man in a brown shirt whom he later recognized as Oswald. A young deputy with the Dallas Police Department also told a story about Oswald leaving. His name was Roger Dean Craig. He identified Oswald in a police lineup after his arrest. He said he watched him coming down the from the knoll and saw him get into a light green Nash rambler station wagon. The vehicle looked like the one that belonged to Ruth Paine. However, while this vehicle was said to look like the car that belonged to Ruth Paine, it had out-of-state license plates. Mrs. Paine's car had Texas license plates.

So, we have three different accounts of how Oswald left the book depository. These stories were told by four different men. These men are, or were, good men who were all known for having outstanding character and who would have had no reason to lie.

There is also the report which was made by two other men who entered the book depository within a minute after the shots were fired. Marion Baker was a motorcycle cop who was escorting the motorcade. He dropped his motorcycle and immediately ran into the building. He encountered Roy Truly, who was the manager of the book depository. Baker and Truly began to search the building together. They arrived together in the lunchroom on the second floor. They encountered a thin young man with brown hair. Officer Baker pulled his gun and pointed it at the man. Then Roy Truly identified the man and said that he worked here in the building. They believe the man in the second-floor lunchroom was Oswald. Both Mr. Truly and Officer Baker said this man had a brown shirt on. This was just ninety seconds after the shots were fired.

On March 20 of 1964, investigators had Marion Baker and Roy Truly retrace their steps. They reenacted their encounter with Oswald in the second-floor lunchroom. A test was done with a stopwatch to see if Oswald could have made it from the sixth-floor sniper's lair to the lunchroom on the second floor in ninety seconds. The first time using a stopwatch, they got one minute and eighteen seconds. The second time it came to one minute and fourteen seconds. The results of this stopwatch test have been used by conspiracy theorists as evidence to support their claim that Oswald was framed. However, both Marion Baker and Roy Truly said Oswald was wearing a brown shirt. Also, Robert McNeil and Pierce Allman believed they had encountered Oswald in the lobby and said he was wearing a brown shirt. Robert McNeil was standing with Sergeant Harkness when witnesses were describing the man whom they saw in the sixth room window with a gun. They all said the man was wearing "a light or white shirt." One of them actually said it looked like a T-shirt and that it was dirty. They said the man they saw was young. It looked to them like he was in his twenties or thirties. They said he was thin and had brown hair. However, they all said the shirt he had on was "white or light." None of them mentioned a brown shirt.

Buell Wesley Frazier told me that the shirt Oswald wore to work that morning had been hanging on a hook under his gray Eisenhower jacket. Oswald would have been wearing a plain white T- shirt at the time of the assassination. Now, Deputy Roger Craig said that this testified that the man had identified as Oswald was wearing a white T-shirt. He said he saw him come down from the grassy knoll and that he got into the back of the light-green Nash rambler station wagon. However, by the time Oswald was outside the building *after* the assassination, he would have had his shirt back on with his Eisenhower jacket over it.

Buell Frazier would have known the real Oswald from an impostor. Oswald was his neighbor and his coworker, and he had been driving him back and forth to work. Deputy Craig identified Oswald as the man he saw get into a light-green Nash rambler when he saw him in a police lineup after he was arrested.

Robert McNeil and Pierce Allman saw a picture of Oswald on the television news after his arrest. Then they recognized him as the man they had encountered in the lobby. So, I believe Buell Frazier's account of how Oswald left the building.

However, this does support my belief that there was a man impersonating Oswald in the book depository on November 22, 1963.

In some of my earlier works, I said the Doorway Man was an Oswald impostor. I knew it couldn't be Oswald himself. I thought they had this man stand in the doorway of the building to provide cover for Oswald. People would think they were seeing Oswald on the front steps of the book depository so they wouldn't suspect him of being in the window on the sixth floor trying to kill the president. Now, I am convinced that the Oswald impostor (or impostors?) was there to provide cover for Oswald so he would be able to slip out the back door undetected.

I didn't want to get into all this controversy about what people said Oswald was wearing when he was reported to have been seen by witnesses in various locations. This evidence is all from the Warren Commission investigation and all public domain. It is all available on the internet. However, the witnesses who described the man in the sixth-floor window said he had a white or light shirt on.

Buell Frazier said that Oswald was wearing a white T-shirt while he was working in the book depository that morning. He watched him put his shirt back on and then put his gray Eisenhower jacket on. He said Oswald left from the rear of the building and went down the steps of the loading platform.

This will help support my position that Lee Harvey Oswald was the shooter in the sixth-floor window. Oswald said that he didn't kill anybody. I believe he told the truth. This does not mean that he wasn't in the window trying to.

Now let's move on to my next chapter.

CHAPTER 7

Roscow White, the Badge Man, and the "I Was Mandarin" Article

In my previous works, I never did get into any discussion about who I believed killed JFK. As of August of 2017, I had it narrowed down to three people. However, I really wasn't sure enough to want to put anything in writing about this.

E. Howard Hunt told his son Saint John that it was a man from the island of Corsica named Lucian Sardi. He was commonly known as Frenchie.

Then a convicted felon named James Files confessed to having killed Kennedy while he was serving time in prison. He told a story about having dropped a shell casing in the dirt behind the stockade fence on the knoll. He said the shell casing would have had his toothmark on it. In 1986, investigators went to this location. They did find a shell casing with a toothmark in it. They said the casing was at a depth in the dirt where it would have been if it had been dropped there in 1963.

Then there is Roscoe White. In August of 2017, when I published the last edition of this book, I knew who Roscoe White was. However, I wanted my book to be short, and therefore I really didn't want to discuss all the people who are linked to this assassination and the evidence of their involvement.

I did know who Roscoe White was. However, what I knew about him was just the information on which had already been researched and exposed by independent researchers and conspiracy theorists.

Apparently, White had served in the marines with Oswald. They found many connections between White and people in Dallas who were linked to the JFK assassination.

I was also aware of the evidence which indicated that Roscoe White was the Badge Man in the famous Polaroid photograph taken by Mary Moorman. There is also a picture which was taken by another photographer of this Badge Man assassin. This image shows him being behind the stockade fence on the knoll. The Moorman photograph shows White behind a cement wall.

Both of these pictures were taken exactly at the same instances that the fatal headshot occurred to JFK. Both photographs have been clarified, colorized, and digitally enhanced. In both pictures, we can clearly see the image of a man wearing a dark-blue policeman's uniform without a hat. We can see that he was a white man with short dark hair. His face was obscured by a white puff of smoke from the weapon he had just fired. These photographs are up on the internet.

Now I am going to be bold enough to say that Roscoe White is going to be the man who actually did kill JFK.

There may have been more than one fatal shot. However, I am convinced beyond a shadow of a doubt that Roscoe White was the man behind the stockade fence who fired the headshot that we see occur at the end of the Zapruder film.

I believe he also fired the wound to Kennedy's throat in the beginning of the assassination. There was an article written by Gary Cartwright that was originally published in the *Texas Monthly* back in December of 1990. Then it was republished in the *National Enquirer* in November of 2017. When I republished my last edition of this book in August of 2017, I did not know about this article. If I had known about this article, I would have used it in my book.

I read this article "I Was Mandarin" when it was republished in the *National Enquirer* in November of 2017. I wish I had known about this sooner.

Roscoe White left a diary for his son Ricky. Prior to finding the diary, Ricky, White Roscoe's son, had been told by someone that his father had been involved with the Kennedy assassination. Roscoe White apparently was a professional targeted killer who was planted in the Dallas Police Department by the CIA. Before I knew this man's name, I believed he was a professionally hired government-trained targeted killer.

I knew about the Badge Man gunman, and I thought that just from the way he handled himself that he was a professional. However, he did leave a diary, but it was stolen by the FBI. Other people saw and read this diary before the FBI took it, besides Ricky.

Also, there is much in the way of photographic, audio, and witness accounts which support the credibility of the information in this diary. There were fifty-eight witnesses who were not called to testify before the Warren Commission.

The famous Washington, DC, attorney Mark Lane went to Dallas and interviewed these people. These films are now videos, which are posted on YouTube.

These people had no way of knowing what Roscoe White had written in his diary. On the other hand, Roscoe White would have had no way of knowing what these witnesses told Mark Lane. There is a consistency between what Roscoe wrote in his diary and what these witnesses told Mark Lane.

So I do believe that the diary Roscoe left for his son Ricky is legitimate. If this diary was a forgery, why would the FBI steal it?

In the beginning of the "I Was Mandarin" article, something caught my attention. Roscoe White's late wife Geneva was talking. She said, "Neither of us slept very well the night before the assassination." She said her husband kept tossing and turning. She finally asked him how he could go through with it. She said Roscoe told her, "Honey, it's like war. The president is a national security threat. If I don't do it, we will be in a nuclear war very soon."

I did not want to republish this whole article in my book. There is just way too much there!

Ricky found his father's diary in 1982. In 1990, Ricky, his mom, and their "team" found a footlocker in the attic of Ricky's grandfather in Paris, Texas.

In addition to other artifacts related to the assassination, they found the naval intelligence cables covered in protective plastic. It was from these cables that Roscoe had received his instructions from the CIA. The cables told Roscoe to drop everything he was doing. He was ordered to go to Dallas.

He was told to take a job on the Dallas police force as an officer. This way he would be in a position to eliminate a "major national security threat and a threat to world peace"—JFK.

This is really going to help me big time. In fact, I believe that Roscoe White is going to come through for me now from beyond the grave. In fact, this guy is going to end up being my new *dead* best friend.

There is a YouTube video interview with Ricky White. The photography expert Robert Groden was there really being supportive of Ricky. Robert Groden is going to be wrong about Oswald being the Doorway Man in the Altgens photograph; however, he is going to be right about everything he has been saying about Roscoe White!

I believe Roscoe White knew that someday what was done in darkness would be brought to light. He knew he was the man who actually did kill Kennedy. He wanted his family to know, and he wanted them to know that there really was a good reason for this.

Gordon Arnold, a witness to the assassination, said he was filming the motorcade from behind the fence in the parking lot on the knoll. Photographic evidence also shows Arnold in the same pictures with the Badge Man. Only he was holding a camera.

Arnold said he felt a shot actually go right past his ear. Then he was confronted by two police officers. He said one pointed a rifle at him and that the man was crying. Another witness also cited a man in a police uniform running through the parking lot carrying a gun. This witness also said the man was crying. This indicates that this JFK assassination is going to be a very sad, tragic event.

This is the conclusion I have drawn from these accounts.

I hope people will enjoy reading this new edition and will learn something they had never thought of before from my analysis of these events.

Pump Up Your Book
The May 2018 Virtual Tour Promotion

A close friend of mine who was a professional author recommended to me that it would be a great idea to have my book promoted by the Pump Up Your Book website. She said she had done promotions for her books through this website, and it had helped her a great deal.

This website is hosted by a woman named Dorothy Thompson. She interviewed me and promoted my book. I believe this interview should still be available on the Pump Up Your Book website.

My book was also reviewed. These reviewers did give me much better reviews than the conspiracy buffs gave my 2007 version of this book on the educational forum in 2009. I did learn from all these reviews, and I kept their feedback in mind when I wrote this new edition over again. I also kept in mind the negative comments that the conspiracy buffs had made about my 2007 edition. I did correct the things I was wrong about and did add much more information to support the case I've been trying to make.

I believe in this new edition; I have done just that.

My Interview on Revolution Radio
Hosted by Robert D. Morningstar,
November 18, 2018

On November 18 of 2018, between 3:00 and 5:00 p.m. I was interviewed by a New York journalist named Robert

D. Morningstar. This interview was one of the most thrilling and exciting experiences of my life. We agreed about many things, yet there were instances when we expressed opposing views. People who had listened to this interview all expressed opinion that it was an interesting dialogue. I had not mentioned the former president George H. W. Bush in my book. I was more than aware of the evidence of his alleged involvement in the JFK assassination. My objective was to try to out poppy Bush. I wanted to see if we could get any comment or reaction from him before he died. Of course, I failed to achieve my objective, as the elder Bush passed away a week and a half later. I was just devastated.

In this interview, I was debating with men who have much more educational and professional credentials than I do. However, my friends who listened to the interview all said that I really held my own with them.

It was an honor to be on the show, and I am very grateful to Robert D. Morningstar for allowing me to express my opinions.

My Blog Posts about the
JFK Plot from 2015
September 17, 2015–October 3, 2015

More of My Thoughts on JFK Plot

It seems that people in the JFK Assassination Community have a real big problem with the evidence of Kennedy's own involvement in his assassination plot. Some of them wouldn't even read my book because I said this. Both the

Warren Report Supporters and the Conspiracy theorists tend to see JFK just as he appeared on television in the early 1960's. They just see his image and what he stood for or represented to them, politically. They have blinded themselves to what was actually going on with him in real life.

Perhaps I didn't get into enough depth and detail about this in my book. I want to explain more fully why these Intelligence officers had some leverage with JFK when it came to getting him to agree to go along with this.

JFK really was a very, very sick man. He had a lot of problems with his physical health. He was apparently in a tremendous amount of pain that he claimed to be constant, and "excruciating." He was also under the influence of a lot of heavy drugs. According to Kennedy, these drugs were impairing his judgment but we're not helping him much with pain management. He probably did not have too much longer to live.

He did dread nuclear war.

It did weigh heavily on his mind throughout his administration. Yet, he ordered things which really would have caused the Soviets to attack the US with nuclear weapons if they had found out that he had ordered these things.

Impeachment resolutions had been introduced in the House of Representatives at the time of his assassination. Apparently, he had an affair with an East German spy and because of the murders of the President and Vice President of South Vietnam. There was going to be a Congressional investigation into his administration. If Kennedy had resigned Congress would have set up committees to investigate him and his administration anyhow. His resignation would have been an admission of guilt.

He really was guilty of serious abuses of the powers of his office. His abuse of power extended out beyond the borders of the United States. This really was not known at the time. However, the tip of the whole iceberg was beginning to surface.

Unbeknownst to the American people at the time, JFK had ordered foreign leaders of other governments assassinated. There were attempts being made on the life of Fidel Castro. There was the massacre of Nu and Diem of South Viet Nam whose deaths he really did order, directly.

Also, there were two other leaders who he had assassinated named Jose Tradjeo and Patrice Lumumba. These were socialist leaders of governments which were supported by the Soviet Union. These were acts of war and violations on International Law which were serious enough for Nuclear War to have been declared on the United States.

These are all commonly known facts today, but in the early 1960's they were guarded top secrets. Even the problem with his affairs and his womanizing wasn't known. At the time of his Presidency, the American people thought they had Prince William and Kate Middleton in our White House here! That's what JFK and Jackie looked like . . . back then. However, what was really going on behind the scenes was something else again. Everyone knows this today!

Anyhow, JFK did have some problems with impaired judgment. He did have weak character development because of how his father brought him up. He was taking large doses of methamphetamine, Nembutal, and other drugs which further impair judgment and cause psychosis ... Then, there was his so-called "zipper" problem. All the casual sex and affairs that he had going on was probably because of a hunger for intimacy. This was because of the psychopathic personality disorder. He also had a male lover named Lem Billings who was with him since they were roommates in the Choate School. I did not get into this in my book.

However, it really would have hurt the country if any of these things had been made known. JFK certainly would not have wanted anyone to find out about these things!

Nevertheless, I am sure these Intelligence Officers came on to him very aggressively. They probably used some undo influence tactics on him. They probably made it quite clear to him that he either had to agree to go this way in Dallas or everyone was going to be toast!

He was in a lot of pain, high on drugs, and he did dread Nuclear War.

So I am sure he said, "By all means, if this is the case then take me out." What did he really have left to live for? He would have been more than agreeable to what these Intelligence Officers asked him to do.

The title of the legal statute the Kennedy assassination is going to come under is called "Government Sponsored Targeted Killing." The kind of cover that the government has on this is called a "Blanket Cover." This is why the Conspiracy Theorists and independent investigators haven't been able to get at any of these people through the conventional legal system.

October 2, 2015

Why They Felt JFK Had to Die by Means of Assassination

My book, "Probable Cause, Rethinking the JFK Plot," was not at all well received by the JFK Assassination Community. Robert D. Morningstar was the first journalist to help me. In November of 2013, he wrote an article in UFO Digest about my book. He titled his article, "Did JFK Deserve to Die?" I want to explain to people why the US Intelligence Community had to "Target Kill" a sitting United States President on Nov. 22 of 1963. He had to die by means of assassination. No other cause of death would have solved the problem that these Intelligence Officers had on their hands.

They could not allow for him to be impeached. They could not have him resign. They couldn't have him die of a stroke or a heart attack. They couldn't even take him sailing and drown him so that it would look like an accident. These Senior Intelligence Officers were in their fifties and sixties in 1963.

They would have remembered something that happened here in 1923 that very few people living today would even know about. President Warren Harding died of a heart attack in August of 1923. He wasn't impeached, nor did he resign. He passed away from a natural cause. Yet, as soon as Harding died, the "Teapot Dome" scandal blew up. Harding's death did not stop Congress from investigating Harding and his administration.

Within a year or two, all the dark stuff came out. Everyone knew about his affairs, his womanizing, his mistresses, his drinking and his gambling, etc. So they knew that if JFK had died from an illness or an accident, Congress would still pursue an investigation into JFK and his administration. Even his death in office would not stop the controversy from starting up. Committees would have been set up and Congress would have launched an investigation into JFK and his administration anyhow. Then, all the dark, sorted, nasty business would have all come out. They could not afford for that to happen.

With the assassination, people would be investigating to find out if Oswald was acting alone or if a conspiracy was involved. It would be at least ten or fifteen years before Congress would launch any investigations into the Kennedy administration. It was only because of the Watergate Scandal that Congress decided to investigate the Kennedy administration. This is when the "dark stuff" started being brought to light. The people in Congress got the idea that there was a connection between the JFK assassination and the Watergate Scandal. There was evidence surfacing as early as 1973 linking people from the Watergate Scandal to JFK Assassination. If it hadn't been for the Watergate Scandal we probably wouldn't know as much as we know about these things today. . . They would have kept them covered up even longer.

October 25, 2015

Why the Conspiracy Theorists Are Helping the Warren Report Supporters

Again, I am blogging some more about the JFK Plot. There are just some things I want to add, and some other things I want to get into some more depth about. There are still a couple of minor things I need to correct.

The Conspiracy Theorists and other JFK researchers are truly brilliant, remarkable people. There is much truth and credibility to the results of their investigations. However, there are some things they are saying that has really been helping the Warren Report Supporters, strengthening them and making them stronger. The Oliver Stone movie "JFK, the story that won't go away," which was made in 1991, was intended to bring the public's attention to the fact that this matter remains unresolved. I agree that the matter does warrant further investigation. My personal is to get the case reopened.

As it is, Oliver Stone and the other Conspiracy Theorists failed in their efforts. In fact, over the past 20 years more people came back to believe the Warren Report. At one time 81% of the people believed there was a conspiracy. Now, it is only 61%. They have not been able to deliver a knockout punch to the Warren Report. In spite of all of their efforts they are losing ground and the Warren Report Supporters are winning.

That's because in some ways they are being their own worst enemies. There are some things they are saying that they are going to be wrong about. Yet, they are still pushing the theories which were presented in the Oliver Stone film.

When they present this information as a criminal conspiracy, and say that the government won't prosecute the people behind it, the Warren Report supporters just trash all their evidence and say they don't have a case. They claim that all the evidence of conspiracy is all conjecture and that it is all contrived.

Believe me, there is just way too much evidence which has surfaced for it to have been falsely made up.

However, the Conspiracy Theorists have been distorting and politicizing this information. They have been insisting that the people who have been linked to this assassination did this on their own, as a crime they committed against this President. They are die-hard certain that these people plotted this assassination for revenge, for money, and to achieve corrupt political objectives of their own. They want to put the responsibility on all these "other people" while they are in complete and total denial of the President's own involvement.

This is where they are helping the Warren Report Supporters and the people in our government who want to keep the cover going.

By presenting this as a criminal case they are hurting our chances of ever learning the truth. I am with them, that we need to get the controversy resolved and have final closure brought to these dark matters of our past.

However, these are covered, above-the-law, clandestine operations of the United States Government. It is futile to try to deal with these things through the conventional legal system. Then, when all their legal efforts fail, it just reaffirms and reinforces the idea that the Warren Report is the truth. So the cover prevails. So we just go round and round, between the Criminal Conspiracy Theorists and the Warren Report Supporters, with the Warren Report Supports still winning.

I believe the government has a thick, deep, wide "Blanket Cover" on a "Government Sponsored Targeted Killing Operation." This is why the Conspiracy Theorists can't get anything done about it through the legal system.

There is a very strict protocol these people have to follow when they do Black Ops, targeted kills, and other above the law operations. They don't just meet in a park somewhere and come up with these ideas and go and carry them out on their own.

November 13, 2015

JFK: Why the Theories That Have Oswald as "Framed" Don't Work

I presented a theory in my book as to how the Kennedy assassination was staged, without actually framing Oswald by planting evidence in the Sniper's lair, or in the car, or on the stretcher. My theory is much more realistic, much simpler, and so much more practical.

The late E. Howard Hunt gave some extensive confessions to his son, Saint John in the three and a half years prior to his death. He admitted that not only was he involved with the JFK assassination, but that he planned it, with David Atlee Phillips and others.

However, he never said that Oswald was framed and didn't fire any shots at all. His confessions indicate that they used Oswald as a gunman and had other gunmen there besides.

This is consistent with my theory that I have been writing since 1980.

If Oswald had been framed, as some conspiracy theorists claim, they wouldn't have needed any other gunmen. They would have had a CIA or perhaps a Mafia hitman steal Oswald's gun from the Paine garage. He would have fired it once, from one location and killed the President instantly.

Then there wouldn't be all this technical controversy. They would have had just one shot and a dead President. They wouldn't have had to do any altering or tampering with the evidence to try to cover up for the other shots.

They would have had a perfect Warren Report with just one single shot.

However, there are a whole lot of things that could have happened that would have blown this whole thing for them, right then and there. Everything would have gone down for them that day. Then there wouldn't have even been a Warren Report.

They might have been caught stealing the gun. They might have been caught planting the evidence. Oswald might have taken his other gun to the Trade Mart luncheon and shot another politician. He could have been packing books in the back of the warehouse where 20 people could have said he was with them. The actor, Charles Bronson, might have stayed a little longer and filmed that sixth-floor window at the time of the assassination, showing nobody was there. Someone else could have. There would have been way to many risks involved.

Other people confessed to having been involved with the Kennedy assassination over the years, including James Files and David Atlee Phillips. They seemed to indicate that Oswald was one of the assassins, and that other gunmen were there besides.

I know there are "Doorway Man Framers" and then there are "Lunchroom Framers." Both are going to be wrong.

However, there is evidence that there were Oswald imposters. There were a lot of Oswald sighting in the days and weeks leading up to the assassination. Also, there were too many reported Oswald sightings in the Book Depository on the morning of the assassination and even after the assassination before his arrest for them all to have been him.

The people behind the assassination used these "Oswald Look-A-Likes" to create confusion and to serve as decoys.

Professor Jim Fetzer, Oregon, Wisconsin, has a passion for his Doorway Man Theory. He writes about this is the

Veterans Today newsletter. He also wrote a book called "Assassination Science." He insists that a photography expert studied the photograph of the Doorway Man and came to the conclusion that the Altgens photograph was altered. He claims that they put superimposed a picture of Billy Lovelady's head onto Oswald's body.

Mr. Altgens was a photographer for Associated Press. He sent that famous Doorway Man photograph out over a photo fax machine. Newspapers and magazines had it within a half an hour after it was taken.

How does Professor Fetzer account for when this photograph was altered? He thinks someone confiscated the camera from Mr. Altgens and took it to a darkroom. Then they just happened to have a picture of Billy Lovelady's head in just the right size. Then they put it on Oswald's body, and gave the camera back to Mr. Altgens, all within a half an hour! The fact is that this Associated Press photographer never let his camera out of his hand.

Robert D. Morningstar told me that it has been proven that the picture was altered while it was being transmitted over a photo fax machine. The year was 1963. Internet had not been invented yet. Neither had digital photography been invented that we have today. If there is any way that a photograph could start out as one picture and end up another one while it was in the process of being transmitted over a fax machine, they would have needed Internet to be able to hack into the Fax machine from the outside. Photographs back then were on film. The only way a picture could be changed would have been in a dark room.

Anyone with any common sense can see that this theory is out in left field and off the deep end. There was a time when I believed the Doorway Man would turn out to be an Oswald imposter. Now I know for sure that this figure in the famous Altgen's photograph was William Nolan Lovelady, AKA: Billy Lovelady.

BIBLIOGRAPHY

Full Text of Roscoe White Archive.org.

Hedegaard, Eric. "The Last Confession of Howard Hunt."

Hersh, Seymour. *The Dark Side of Camelot*. Back Bay Books, 1998.

Hunt, E. Howard. *Undercover*. Berkley Publishing Company, 1974.

Hunt, Saint John. *Bond of Secrecy*. Trine Day Publishing, 2012.

"I Was Mandarin," *The Texas Monthly*, December 1990

Republished in *The National Enquirer* November 2017.

Marchetti, Victor. Liberty Lobby Article, "Jury: CIA Involved in JFK Assassination." 1985.

National Geographic. "Was Kennedy Tied to The Mob?" October 23, 2013.

New York Post. "The Kennedy Meth." 2013.

"One Man's Encounter with Oswald," JFKfacts.org.

Phillips, David Atlee. *Night Watch*. Ballantine Books, 1982.

Powers, Thomas. *Richard Helms: The Man Who Kept the Secrets*. Knopf, 1979.

Shaw, Mark. *The Poison Patriarch: How the Betrayal of Joseph R. Kennedy_Caused the Assassination of JFK*. Skyhorse Publishing, 2016.

Summers, Anthony. *Conspiracy*. McGraw Hill, 1980.

The United States Government. The Warren Report. 1964.

The Warren Commission Testimony, 1964.

ABOUT THE AUTHOR

Robin Haines was born in Jersey City, New Jersey, on March 20, 1953. Her mother was a journalist for a newspaper called the *Hudson Dispatch*, which later became the *Jersey Journal Dispatch*. She was a religion editor who also covered theater and entertainment and occasionally covered stories about politics. Her father was a wine salesman who eventually became a cab driver. Both of her parents are now deceased.

She graduated from Weehawken High School in June of 1972. She attended Manhattan School of Music and also to some extension courses at Julliard in theory and composition but did not obtain a degree.

She resided in Weehawken, New Jersey, until she was twenty-nine. Then she relocated to Winchester, Virginia, where she still lives today. She has never been married.

Her many interests include politics, religion, military, and American history. She also enjoys horseback riding, theater, and current events.

Her personal goal is to have the cover removed from the JFK Operation so the whole truth can finally be established.

There is a question etched in stone on the wall of the National Archives in Washington, DC. It reads "Those who don't remember the past are bound to repeat it." The United States government and the American people have been repeating many of its past mistakes and even making worse ones because so much of the truth about our nation's past has been withheld from them.

The author deeply believes that the many controversies, which are still hanging over us from the 1960s and 70s, need to be resolved. Final closure should be brought to these things while there are still some people living who have firsthand knowledge of them.

She hopes that out of all this tragedy, some new laws and treaties will be passed, one of which will require that all public figures seeking election to the presidency and vice presidency of the US must be subject to a top-secret national security background check for the highest level of clearance. This would definitely serve as a deterrent to prevent a situation like this from arising here again. People seeking election to the high public office need to be screened much more carefully for character flaws, mental health, and for ties to foreign governments and extremist political organizations. The American people also need to come to have a better understanding of what is meant by national security, civil defense, and politics.

She also wants people throughout the world to decide to commit to achieving the goal of abolishing all nuclear weapons. We do need to get rid of them.

www.ingramcontent.com/pod-product-compliance
Lightning Source LLC
Chambersburg PA
CBHW031311060726
47590CB00003B/1155